HEAT

T0362592

Series 3 Number 6

Julian Hooper
Precocious Alphabet 2022
acrylic on canvas
40 × 35 cm

Julian Hooper recalls drawing
alphabets as a child, influenced by
seventies posters and Speedball
Textbooks (a resource for sign writers
and calligraphers since the early
twentieth century).

This painting, first exhibited as
part of *Mark Work* at Objectspace
Auckland, builds each letter out of
both upper and lower case forms,
creating a new version of each letter.

FIONA WRIGHT
TO BEGIN / IT BROKE

Fiona Wright is a writer, editor and critic from Sydney. Her book of essays *Small Acts of Disappearance: Essays on Hunger* won the 2016 Nita B. Kibble Award and the Queensland Literary Award for non-fiction, and was shortlisted for the Stella Prize and the New South Wales Premier's Literary Awards. Her first poetry collection, *Knuckled*, won the 2012 Dame Mary Gilmore Award, while *Domestic Interior* was shortlisted for the 2018 Prime Minister's Literary Award for Poetry. Her most recent book of essays is *The World Was Whole*.

TIME, I KEPT HEARING PEOPLE SAY THAT YEAR, has broken. Time broke: as if it were an object knocked from a shelf, or an ancient, stuttering machine with parts worn through.

I'm getting ahead of myself already.

Time is a function of narrative.

There are so many places where this all begins, undoubtedly more besides. Beginnings are never obvious or unequivocal, even at the best of times; it's only after they have happened that we can even think to notice them. Consequence in search of a causality. It takes time to order time.

Neuroscience has the term 'postdiction' for something like this, a prediction in reverse. And the term exists because it is fundamental to the brain's continual operation. It is how the brain reckons with the physical world, moment by moment, how we perceive. The brain suspends itself. For a brief moment, it suspends itself until all of the disparate information of the body's many senses can filter in; it suspends us, or it suspends the world, or it suspends time. And only then does it begin interpretation, making sense of the moment about one-twelfth of a second after the moment itself has passed.

Everything we perceive comes to us by way of postdiction (and what or where it is that we are for the duration of that fraction of a second I can't begin to guess at). It is built into our bodies, and all our narratives depend on it as well.

We always were and always are operating out of sync.

So perhaps the best place to begin is in the middle of things, in the present or somewhere close to it. Time has broken: I'm still hearing this phrase, more than two years since I first encountered it at the beginning of the pandemic. Time has broken: I know that it stood out to me because I felt it too, but I still don't know, exactly, how to qualify that, or even what the words actually mean. Time broke, but no one seems able to explain precisely how, or why.

The time I feel or occupy or seem to *have* (how can we have a thing that we can neither hold nor hold on to?) is behaving differently; I can't account for it in the same way. I can't rely on it to turn up consistently, the way it used to; on its regular progression, its steady clockwork (so to speak). It isn't present (so to speak) in the same way. I miss it, and I can't quite get it back.

The shift did happen somewhere in these last pandemic years, though I'm not sure if that is cause or just coincidence. It wasn't the lack of structure in an at-home working day or the limits placed on movement that could have made time break for me – I'm used to these, and have been, by now, for years. What changed for me instead was that so much of my day-to-day solitude, that stretch of hours every day spent on my own, fell away, entirely and suddenly. My housemates were also home, suddenly, across those weekday work days that I'm so used to drifting through alone, the local parks and supermarkets and (now takeaway) cafés were, perversely, busier; and time too felt more full. And then somewhere in there, somewhere in those first, strange months I fell in love, and this too happened unexpectedly and accidentally; this too is an experience that always alters the texture and the breadth of time, its attenuation.

By the time we had moved in to this 'living with' phase of the pandemic (another nonsensical phrase) I had moved in with this woman. Or more precisely, we moved in together, into a narrow house that sits partway over an old laneway for carriages and rattles at its core, sometimes, with passing traffic. I have never lived with a partner before, or even come particularly close, and so I didn't know (I couldn't know) the different feel of time without plans – those interspersed staying-in evenings and quiet weekends, the ones I've always spent alone – when these too would be by default accompanied. This isn't always an active keeping of company, of course – often each of us is in a different room reading or working or pottering about (she calls this 'pootling') wordlessly– and it's lovely. There's a comfort to this, a respite, and a sense, somehow, that I'm less insubstantial to myself, and all of these things I never imagined I might find at all, and certainly not like this. Nor that some of that loneliness, so silent and submerged I hardly ever felt the ache of it, might ever drain away.

But time moves differently when we are with other people than it does when we're alone. We perceive it differently, misjudge durations: it feels faster, more fluid, less likely to catch or stick. There's growing evidence that our time perception recalibrates in social settings, that it somehow moves towards convergence, towards a shared time, with whomever we are sharing our time. Time that's spent in solitude takes fewer cues from other people, from anything external, and we are pulled from its interiority less frequently. Time in solitude sometimes has a density as a result that I have always loved; and since the pandemic, since I have been spending so much less time in this state, time has lost its tack. Time has quickened, and it will not slow back down.

In my worst moments (though these too pass more quickly) I sometimes think: I knew I didn't get to have this. I always knew.

Precisely what *this* is, though – comfort, companionship, intimacy and its sense of sharedness, simply love – this I still don't know. There's so much that I never expected and still can't quite comprehend.

And it is hard to find a footing when even time has changed. Or it is hard to find a footing because even time has changed.

Time is a function of gravity, and its swifter movement always indicates a weaker pull.

The simplest place to begin, perhaps, is by way of change. Change, that is, is the simplest definition (it's not simple) of time that we have, and the one that scientists have come closest to agreeing upon (they do not agree): time is the occurrence of change. (Some add, *sequentially*.)

When you're older you will. You're still too young to. My sense of time had already been changing, much more slowly and gently, in a way that I have realised has something to do with scale. It takes time to learn a sense of time that has duration. Time that endures. And to understand what I know my younger selves could not – that I had time, and would have time; and didn't have to throw myself upon it with such urgency and need.

It has something to do too with having accrued enough time to have witnessed or experienced changes, both the superficial and the momentous, to have seen and felt something of time's dynamism. Of the constant, quiet transformations of the world, and all that is remade, and then remade again.

What I'm saying is: it's only recently that I have seen begin to dissipate some of the forces that have long been at work across my life, that have pressed their shape upon what I've experienced and the means by which I have been able to configure a self (constant, quiet, continually remade). The wonder and the hope of that feels miraculous, all the more so because I don't know how these kinds of changes happen, how ideas and political climates and cultural norms shift about with time. I don't think anyone really does, at least not until after the fact (hindsight abhors chaos, the unruly). But in recent years the world I was born into has stopped feeling immutable or entrenched, or even ahistorical. It's only recently I've understood this as a function of time, its transfigurations.

So many of the stories I have read about time begin with a moment of misrecognition. Where a character catches a glimpse of their face or body in an unexpectedly reflective surface, and is surprised to find it changed, and so profoundly. Who is this old man, they think, or, when exactly did this happen, or, oh my god, I see my mother in my mirror. What disturbs them is the stark reminder that they carry within themselves an image of their body that is outdated, that other people do not see or know. But what I've always found strange is that it is this earlier version of their body and face, the one unmarked and unchanged, that they almost always consider to be the more accurate reflection of who they truly are – even though it is this body, the youthful body, that is (was) the body they had not shaped or earned.

I've never really understood the crisis these moments so often represent, the hurt and loss and desperation they elicit in these characters. Misrecognition doesn't surprise me, and it is undramatic because it happens for me every day. A quick flash of it, each morning when I first see my face in the bathroom mirror, because it is a thing I have forgotten overnight.

This too is unremarkable: the inability to remember faces is a difference in the brain far more prevalent than most people suspect (mostly because of how quickly and unconsciously we learn to find and use other markers of identity, without knowing that there's any other way). Each morning I know that the face that looks back is my own; logic, or even just past experience, accounts for that. It just never quite appears the way that I expect to (although exactly what it is I am expecting, I also do not know). Misrecognition does not speak for me of time's unrelenting, existential pull, of all that's passed and irretrievable, as it does for these characters. It is daily, ordinary, simple-present time that I see here instead. Continuity rather than crisis.

Time is a function of change – but change is a function of comparison.

What I do notice, or notice instead: because the faces of my friends are also new to me each time I see them, they don't (or can't) ever appear to be getting any older. Instead, it seems that younger people are somehow all a little younger every year.

It is the body that ties us to time, with the body that we apprehend and understand it: the body may well be where this all begins.

One of my teenage fascinations, wonderfully intense, was with forensics, and those tiny traces that the body leaves as it moves through the world, everything it sheds, what might be betrayed this way. A book was to blame, as is even now often my way – that I had never encountered the concept before was understandable then, because it was still another year or two before every police procedural on TV seemed to turn at once in that direction. In each story, it was a single, minute piece of matter that led the detectives almost directly to the killer (the cases were all murders, the murdered were all women, the more things change and all that). A sliver of skin beneath a fingernail, one hair left clinging to a cushion or jacket. I spent months taking casts of footprints in my backyard using junk-shop plaster of Paris without ever actually succeeding in lifting one free.

What compelled me here, I know, was that sense of the body pressing up against the world and leaving something of itself behind at every point of contact (even then I didn't feel my own substantiality); but also of the body bearing traces, concretely, of that unshareable and secret self it carries somewhere within (even then I didn't feel my visibility). What might this way be revealed of the person in the body: their interests, interactions, comforts, what they make and what they love. I read about coal miners and their absorbed streaks of silvery blue mineral dust embedded in their hands and fingers, about the bony protrusions and breakages in the feet of ballet dancers, the microorganisms on the skin of people who have pets or plants or rising damp or air conditioners, different causes of different scars. The calluses particular to cycling, sewing, sanding, or writing by hand, to weightlifters, cleaners, ceramicists and pastry chefs, cellists and saxophonists, and many kinds of nurses.

Almost all of these traces, I realise now, are accruals of one kind or another. These are marks made over time and by time; and if they are evidence of anything, above all else they are evidence of time.

All of that time, borne in and by the body: I know that back then, that much time was unfathomable, mysterious enough to not feel completely real. No teenager can comprehend all of that time – how a decade, much less a lifetime, might feel or be understood. No teenager can comprehend this kind of accumulation, each single, simple, unremarkable action in repetition across so many years. What I felt of time, at that time – I remember this so keenly – was desperate impatience, a frustration all but twitching in my muscles. I burned with it. When you're older you can. You're still too young for. Give it time.

I've known for some years now that my body would wear its accruals sooner than most, would be marked earlier, and marked more. It doesn't bother me the way I thought it would; at least, it doesn't yet. There are three reddened lumps that always sit across my right-hand knuckles, each year growing bigger and more bruise-like at the onset of winter, then shrinking back again when it begins to warm. There's a hard knot of sinew wedged up behind my shoulder blades, an unfocus that creeps into my vision when I'm tired; my ears sting under any kind of pressure where a ridge of extra bone has grown, protectively. The immutability of these changes astounds me, sometimes, but I don't have the sense that any of this is loss. If anything, it feels like ownership, an unexpected possession: my ears sting from all the slap-cold air I've walked through, in wind-funnelling cityscapes, along coastlines, at night in winter; my shoulder stiffens exactly where I've arced myself back a little, to better look into the faces of all the taller people I have talked to; the reading and writing that fills my days has tired my eyes. The blood supply to my knuckles and toes has been inconsistent for years, faltering each time I've been unable to take in enough fuel for my body to attend to its extremities.

All of these ways we live with and through time. I didn't know, back then, that these accruals, these markings, might not speak only of that hidden person in my body but would also, somehow, reveal my body to my person, as part of me and as my

16

own. I didn't know that they could offer this assurance. Duration is always an endurance of some kind.

And then there's the obvious place to begin, close to where we all begin: here are some children.

Here are some children: that's how the sudden presence of my girlfriend's two small children in my life has often felt. I've never wanted children of my own, never imagined having all that much to do with them, apart from in the role of an eccentric aunt (I firmly believe that everyone needs one of these). But even if this desire was one I'd ever felt (or even briefly entertained), I know I wouldn't have imagined their appearance in my life so soon or at such speed. I'd never had cause, that is, to contemplate what this might look like or mean. And I'd certainly never thought to consider that the company of children would bring me so often and so immediately into contact with my own childhood. That I would find myself remembering so much that I'd not thought about for years, and feeling it, exquisitely, afresh.

Time is a function of memory.

Last year my girlfriend bought her kids a new game for their Nintendo – a brilliant, kooky game with that single but fatal flaw of being single-player without saying as much on the box. The boys agreed to take fifteen-minute turns; I set a timer on my phone while my girlfriend oversaw the coin-toss. And for fifteen minutes, the younger brother watched the elder play, reflexively twitching and jolting alongside as if it were his body running and leaping on the screen, and beset by enemy chickens, all but falling from the couch in his excitement. He was six then, only just. When the timer rang, he pounced on the controller within an instant. When it rang again, fifteen minutes later, he was nothing short of aggrieved. I have never seen such wounded outrage in the flesh.

What did you do? he cried out, and, why did you *change* it? I didn't, at first, understand. He wouldn't be assuaged by any of my assurances that I'd not touched a thing; he knew, he said, just *knew* that I had changed the timer's settings, and he knew it because the fifteen minutes that had preceded his turn had been so much longer than the fifteen minutes that had just passed, in which the console had been there in his hands.

And how exactly do you explain relativity to a six-year-old? I'd say whenever I told this story in the weeks that followed, with over-egged despair. In truth, though, his brother did it for us in that moment. Already stabbing away at the controller, and for some reason hanging upside-down from the arm of his chair, he simply called out over (under?) his shoulder, Time flies when you're having fun, my man.

Time is a function of novelty. Time is a function of attention. It is for these reasons that this truism is true.

In hindsight – that strange and powerful gift of time – it seems obvious that the presence of these children would shake loose my own, old history, leave it rattling about again within my brain. Obvious, now, that I have seen the way that their encounters with a new idea or unknown word, their turnings over of a new question in their minds (it's almost visible, sometimes) so often leads me to remember that first grappling of my own, the way the workings of my known world had, each time, so slightly realigned. Or that their as-yet-unhideable emotions, so large on their small faces, can hurtle my own heart back in time. There is a terror to this that I could not have expected, one that comes

18

from knowing how much of childhood persists within any adult, how many injuries and unanchored memories we carry with us into our adult lives, and understanding how often and easily these never-forgotten incidents are caused by simple distraction or inattention, inopportune timing, or accident. I could not have know that the hurtling backwards would sometimes, somehow, catapult me forward too in counterforce: when I can't help but anticipate the adult men these lovely boys will one day become, nor what exactly it might be that I'll unwittingly have given them that bruises, still, when touched.

A friend recently told me that she hated being a child. She hated the choicelessness of childhood, how little of her life she could determine for herself. I told her that what I remember most is my confusion, how much there seemed to be that I just didn't understand. Give it time, I remember adults telling me, in time you'll understand. When you're older you will. You're still too young to. These things are true, of course, but never all that useful.

There is one other phrase I heard so often in the early months of the pandemic: that things like this were *not supposed to happen*. Here too it was incongruence that made it stick with me – nothing is supposed to happen, just as nothing is preordained or inevitable (aside from death and taxes), or predictable in any real way. I don't think the problem is that we do not know this – we speak of the future as uncertain, an unknown country, dark – but even still we tend to imagine it, mostly, as resembling the present (except with better tech). As a continuation of the world that is. The pandemic was not this kind of future; it was outside the scope of our conjecture and imagined possibilities.

What broke, I sometimes think, may well have been this sense of a future unruptured.

But this too was already getting rickety. We were already beginning, just, to try and reckon with a future that's untethering, with all that climate change might render unrecognisable in the world; that the pandemic also felt, at times, like an eruption from an era past certainly did not help at all. Nothing is inevitable, but that time would flounder in these circumstances must come close.

Time broke, I keep thinking, out of all the ways we had been trying to contain it, but it had never really been anything other than wild. It's easy to forget this, I think, because there is so little in this world that is unfathomable like this, that refuses. Some things we don't or can't see properly until they break. And even then, most obvious is the loss.

HANNE ØRSTAVIK
SPRING NIGHT

Translated by Martin Aitken

Hanne Ørstavik published the novel *Cut* in 1994 and embarked on a career that would make her one of the most remarkable and admired authors in Norwegian contemporary literature. Her literary breakthrough came three years later with the publication of *Love*, which in 2006 was voted the sixth best Norwegian book of the last twenty-five years in a prestigious contest in *Dagbladet*. Since then, the author has written several acclaimed and much-discussed novels and received a host of literary prizes. Her fifteenth novel, *Ti Amo*, was published in English in September.

Martin Aitken's translations of Scandinavian literature are numerous. His work has appeared on the shortlists of the 2017 Dublin Literary Award and the 2018 US National Book Awards, as well as the 2021 International Booker Prize. For his translation of Hanne Ørstavik's *Love* he received the 2019 PEN America Translation Prize.

'THE WHOLE HOUSE FELT DIFFERENT because both father and mother were away.' So begins *Spring Night*, a 1954 novel by Tarjei Vesaas, one of the most important of all Norwegian writers.

What does it mean, to write?

What can be written when father and mother are away?

I remember the relief when either mamma or pappa weren't home. They were never away together at the same time. When pappa was away it was tinned meatballs or fast food for dinner and there was nothing to be afraid of, but the fear would come back when pappa came back. (Fear was the two of them home at the same time, at night when the girl lay in her bed, the fear that he might kill mamma for not answering him. When answering him would have been so very easy, if only she'd wanted to. Why wouldn't she answer him. And the knife of that fear cut to the bone, as deep as into death, into there not being anything any more. Why don't you just answer him.) Over a period of several years, mamma would go away once a month, travelling from Tana to Oslo where she was involved in drawing up a proposal for a new Social Services Act. At least when mamma was away there was no trouble (hissing, shouting, kicking, hitting, throttling). But pappa could get so angry and it was hard to know when it would come or why.

I'm beginning to understand that I've lived nearly all my adult life, if not my entire life, in fact, with no adult inside me. That inside I'm a multitude of children, little girls, and that they're all on their own. There's never been an adult there for them. They've remained stuck there in their various positions or situations and have no idea I'm grown up. I've started lying down on the floor for a while in the afternoons, and I close my eyes and try to get to know them. To look at them. I ask them what they're doing, what their tasks have been. I let them see that I'm a woman now, fifty-two years old. I ask them too if there's anything they need.

Very often they need something soft. To sit on a lap and have their hair, their backs, gently smoothed. They want me to handle them very softly, very sensitively. To listen with my hands and allow their small bodies to decide what they want. Even the one who's always facing away in a black leather jacket/hoodie sort of thing with the hood up so that I never see her, even she wants a lap to sit on and will snuggle up to me, full of sadness, and sometimes crying. And I see that she's protecting another, smaller girl, who sits quite unknowingly, *oblivious*, in a meadow while picking flowers, her hands so soft and small.

And I think that writing is language opening up this particular world as a real world among all possible worlds. In Vesaas's *Spring Night*: the world of softness and sensitivity that's inside Olaf, a boy of fourteen, is where everything that happens to the characters in that novel is thrown into relief. In the softness and sensitivity inside him, it's all thrown into relief in the form of inklings, moods, displacements. Olaf sees and sees, without always knowing what it is that he sees, he just sees that something holds or exists, and then it doesn't, or else it changes.

I'm interested in *the remarkable fluidity of our everyday language* – not the language we use to elaborate concepts, to pin down and keep things apart, but the language that brings out what happens when something is uttered by means of everyday words, the way that opens up new and different spaces of experience. I tell myself this is how Vesaas wrote too. He doesn't pin down, but leaves alone whatever is, a mood, an inkling, that melts into another – and both are equally true, a part of a whole, them both – and we're taken there and allowed in, because he is with us.

What is it that fills language out for us, so that it doesn't feel empty? So that something's there?

It's 4 January 2022 and one and a half years since Luigi died. I haven't written anything since what became *Ti Amo*, and that was in January two years ago, when he was still here. Luigi was alive then. And I was writing.

Writing has for me always been the way I came into contact with my emotions. How things feel. By writing things I was able to feel them.

But since Luigi died it's as if my language has been put away in cotton wool inside a bubble of air with a white mist around.

And now suddenly it becomes clear to me that there's something I've passed by: the moment of death.

Per Olov Enquist writes about it in his *The Parable Book*, his friends standing there on the riverbank, that's how he describes it, his friends who are soon to die, they're all soon to die, and he has conversations with these friends of his in what he writes, as they stand on the riverbank. And shortly they'll be going over to the other side.

Luigi lay in our bed, and I sat beside him eating a yoghurt, because I'd just come back from the gym; he made gurgling sounds when he breathed and had blood and slime in his mouth, but he was alive and it was so unthinkable that he was going to die. Even though I knew he was going to die; he'd been medicated into a sleep and I knew he wasn't going to wake up from it. He wasn't standing on a riverbank, he was with me and it was completely natural that I was sitting there with him, I didn't want to eat that yoghurt anywhere else, I wanted to be there, with him.

And then suddenly he was quiet. And it felt so good, it didn't occur to me that he was dead, all I thought was that now at last he could sleep for a bit. It wasn't possible to think that he was dead. There was no riverbank, and no other side. He was alive. And then he went quiet. But he was still there.

I realise now that I haven't *taken it in*, that moment of death. It's as if I jump over it and then I'm on the other side too, where he's dead. I haven't really *immersed* myself in it. Haven't allowed myself to feel it – that he was here, and then wasn't. That moment, a knife gouging a hole in what used to be *us*. Him being with me. Us being together.

Gouging a hole into what's underneath, the nature of which is unknown to me. And which I realise now I haven't allowed myself to become sufficiently *immersed in* to feel. As if I've jumped over his death to the other side, not the other side of death, but the other side of my life, my days. Jumped over to him not existing any more. Is that it?

And I'm asking myself this now because I think it has a bearing on my writing. The fact that there's so much I'm not feeling. Because I'm scared. Because I don't know. And how can I write then?

It's tied up too with the devastating angst that hit me once it fully sank in and I had to acknowledge that he was dead. That angst is ancient and has to do with things that go way back and are stiffened and frozen, and how can I write about that if it's all unimaged, the only pictures in my mind being fleeting glimpses of young girls all alone with no one there, turned away, dressed in black, shutting out. No. Everything hinges on the no. The shrinking away from feeling, perceiving, because there's no rear wall to anything, no bottom to it, and no one holding. And maybe death is there too, my death, decomposition, turmoil, though it feels more frightening than death, because death has a name, a person can say *death*, but what's there, in that hole, has no name, has nothing, is nothing, only falling, and emptiness without end.

(If you want some dick, you can have mine)

Jump across, and he's dead. No stopping to feel, no falling down into the hole where the knife has been. A person can't *immerse themselves* in something that won't hold, that has no bottom to it. What is that?

But can I write if I jump across?

Something else: what borders on the other, the other side, not death but the other side of what we call real, through which Olaf keeps passing, backwards and forwards, in and out.

The faces that come too close, making them distorted, frightening, or unfathomable; pappa took his patients from the psychiatric ward on camping trips with us, we all slept in a big army tent, my brothers too, and the dog, the girl I was then, and we made a fire and the tent was dark inside, and there, from the shadows he comes, a man, small and weak, skinny, he comes right up close and whispers to the girl, ten or eleven years old, softly, as if saying something without weight or not saying anything at all, *If you want some dick, you can have mine*, which didn't frighten the girl but confused her and made her feel proud at the same time. (Blushful because it made her proud, as if she'd been handed a gift and no one was allowed to see she'd been handed a gift because she wasn't worth any gift, but someone had given her one anyway). But the fact they could come out of the half-light in that way, unpredictably, and that it wasn't the patients who were dangerous, what was dangerous was inside her. And that it was so *on the verge*, one thing or another. And what if there was no boundary and there was no difference, and no one holding, anywhere.

How do you open up the place where feelings are? How do you become living? Terror, an iron ring inside the collarbone, weighing down, pressing, making everything so tight and narrow. The little sadist girl inside her, gripping her throat, *strangling* and grinning, squeezing harder. What is it she's protecting her from, keeping her away from?

And the fact that the psychiatric patients were never as frightening as mamma; they were clear and well-defined, it was obvious when they were up to something, it made sense somehow that the one with the dick was always whispering, something about a microphone; anyway, there was always the option of jumping off the bridge into the river, that was something to sling out, something to put out there, but mamma never put anything out there, there was nothing to put, there was nothing in her eyes that said anything or didn't say anything, all there was was a surface, and everything that was inside the girl who was me and which was dangerous came not from mamma but from me, and so there was no place to go there, everything just reflected back, there was nothing in those eyes that absorbed anything that could be processed and sent back out again in a different shape, and maybe it was like that from the very beginning, I think to myself; here I am fifty-two years old, lying on the floor trying to be *constructive* with myself, maybe it was like that right from when I was born, maybe even before that, because she didn't want another child straight afterwards, pappa told me so, she wasn't ready, she'd only just turned twenty-three and already had my brother and was focused on him and her own life which at last was about to begin, and there wasn't even a baker's shop or street lights where we lived up in Finnmark, it was completely dark and you couldn't ever get a loaf of bread anywhere.

And this is no complaint. It's just an attempt – well, to what? To grasp hold of something. To understand.

Acceptance to write the way you have to, the way that it's necessary for you to write – no one can give me that. I think it's part of the courage of writing too, or the struggle of it, or its wonderful joy – that now at last it's possible to do it just the way I want to. The way *I* must and will. Vesaas has his own way of doing it, he glides in his sentences, allows his moods to glide, pursues the nuances and allows them to become what's important, what's visible, that which *is*, and which causes something to change:

Then Gudrun laid her hand on his arm, and he thought she looked so wonderful standing there in her nightgown that he went along with her in accepting Karl.

that he went along with her in accepting

Gudrun came out, she was pale and quiet. Olaf had never seen anything so beautiful as she was when she was pale and quiet. He caught her eye and was allowed to.

and was allowed to

In both these passages, beauty opens out. *She looked so wonderful standing there in her nightgown...Olaf had never seen anything so beautiful as she was when she was pale and quiet.*

What is it about beauty opening out?

There are different layers of beauty here, as well as the beauty that opens out inside us as readers too, because we are the beauty in Vesaas's writing, we are in the soft, soft approach to life that's possible only when something is seen with, what – *love*?

I've always thought there's a tenderness in beauty.

And that tenderness, that softness and sensitivity, is the most vulnerable thing we have and are. But it's also where we're most open. The people in *Spring Night* are each alone, but at the same time, to a smaller or greater extent, open to each other, and where there are openings there are ways of *reaching*. And if something can be reached, it can be touched; we can be changed, perhaps transformed. Set free?

Reading *Spring Night*, and sensing that it was written in the exact way that makes exactly this visible to us and real, and allowed to exist in the world: *that he went along with her in accepting.*

Because it's *said that way.*

The shame (my own) of not being able to make it work better. Of not *being* better. *The shame of this being all there is.*

In my notebook this morning I wrote:

Is it true?

Am I writing truthfully?

Am I in touch with what actually matters?

Began the Vesaas essay Monday, yesterday finished reading *The*

Parable Book / P.O. Enquist – and I know that what I wrote was coloured by it and I feel shame – I want to be free – to feel myself to be strong and free and *unique* when I write – but am grateful too, because reading Enquist again took me back to myself – to the Hanne who writes – pricked a hole in the airbag around the heart that stops me from feeling – I still *feel* nothing but I'm closer now. Now I know a bit about what the question is. From there it's all about carrying on.

('But who would we be if we did not try.')

I think about what it is that happens in our lives when we get older, the way we can still keep going regardless of things that happened to us before, things that hurt or damaged us, but then something happens when we get to forty, and becomes especially obvious to us once we pass fifty, which is that the speed of life we knew when we were young isn't there any more to carry us forward, our animal, physical will for life becomes worn, our wounds seem as if to weep, and at once we're there in the midst of it, that vanilla life, and we struggle and strive and are barely capable of keeping our heads above water any more.

I always think about Whitney Houston, who in her voice seemed to *carry everything*, love's whole weight, the entire will for it to actually last and withstand, *I will always love you*, that long, long note when the song lifts towards the end, and yet it doesn't end there at all, it can't end on that voice, it holds and prevails. Only then is doesn't hold at all, it won't bear anything any more, Whitney Houston dies alone of an overdose in the bath of a Beverly Hills hotel room, I picture the long corridors with wall-to-wall carpeting, flecks of dust dancing in the light, and I think to myself that there was no one there in that room to hold her in her song, no adults watching out for her.

At the moment of Luigi's death I became orphaned again (angst).

In my novel entitled *Novel. Milan,* a young woman of twenty-seven I call Val meets an older man, Paolo, and what she yearns for (her parents abandoned her when she was three) is someone to belong with, someone to whom she feels connected and can come home to, someone she can belong *to.* The novel blends the city and its architecture, inside and outside, film, dream, fantasy; it's a very pictorial novel in that way, I think, every section is a picture with a title, because a picture can *speak,* as a picture, it doesn't need to *say everything,* the way concepts or words do, the words are required to make the picture emerge, but it's *in the picture* that everything happens, that's where the words become real.

In my notebook I wrote this too: Am I scared of writing? Scared of not being real any more – that what I write isn't real – all the men I sleep with in the bed where Luigi died (the moment of death I won't *immerse myself in*) – when I drink in the evenings – who am I?

Where is the adult in me then?

Has everyone gone away?

And I think: How can I be sincere when I don't know what I feel? I can ask others if they feel anything in their chests – can you feel anything there? Can you feel your own love, in the area around the heart?

Because obviously it's not the case that I *can't* feel. I've already written about this – I know I can feel, I've just got no access to it as feeling. I don't *feel* it. I can see it. I can write it. But I can't feel it in my body.

In fact, I can sense this in my body, only not as feeling, not as such. I can go really weak behind my left knee, and then I know something nasty or overwhelming is going to happen to me. It's like someone whacking my knee from behind, a stabbing pain, as if to make me submit, give in. For a time after I got divorced and moved back to the city with my daughter, who had to change schools, when everything was up in the air, I'd walk with her part of the way along Ruseløkkveien every morning, not all the way to the school gates, but turning back in the other direction before we got there and walking up to Frognerparken before going home again to write. And every morning when I got to the park entrance or had just gone in, my ankles would give way. I couldn't stand up any more and would have to sit down on the ground. I'd be sitting there for a while, and then after a bit I'd be able to get up again and carry on. And I knew there was nothing wrong with my legs, I knew it had to do with feelings, only I couldn't feel them, apart from like that, my ankles going wobbly and giving way, and all I could do was sink to the ground and stay there a while.

But what's hardest is that I don't feel anything when I'm with others. I know I've *got* feelings, I just can't feel them. *The Blue Room*, from 1999, ends in, 'I see the reflection of my own eyes in hers. And feel nothing.'

During the autumn and early winter I've been reading Ali Smith's Seasonal Quartet, and it's the way she has of being so free, the way she moves through time and structures, the way *everything is real* in those books, even the unreal is real, someone's death can talk and hide away in a tree trunk, a disembodied head can sleep beside you on your pillow and talk to you when you wake up; a little girl can get through the guarded perimeters of a refugee detention centre and *be heard*.

And I ask myself: What is it about Ali Smith that makes her so free?

I don't know – but I do know a few things about her, like that she's gay, in a relationship (with Sarah, I think, to whom she always dedicates her books); she has passed sixty years old now, and is not just a Brit, but a Scot, which means she's from the periphery.

I think maybe it's all about everything going against conventions (gay, older) – and being with someone in a relationship can be a way of freeing yourself up, because that's something that can make you feel secure, someone being there who can hang on to you, you can let go and fall and it'll be all right – and I think that writing and life hang together and that if you've got access to all that in your life, then maybe you've got access too to those sorts of dimensions in your writing. It's definitely worth thinking about as a hypothesis. Of course, I ask myself at what point I, Hanne, start pulling in the other direction. The most obvious place to begin is with my body. It's completely impossible for me to imagine myself not being thin. This thing with my body is something I've yet to fully understand, but I know it has to do with love. Am I wantable if I'm not thin any more, if I no longer can feel the bones in my body? And I know too that it has to do with that other thing as well, being able to access one's feelings. My feelings are in my body. It means I can't get through to them. I keep my body on a short rein. Am I then keeping my feelings back too? Body shape. Would I be writing differently if I allowed myself to put on weight? And: the fact that the very idea is just totally, totally, totally impossible. Why?

But how do I get to allowing myself to *immerse*? I don't know. But I do know something. At the moment I'm focused on a way of understanding our inner world that doesn't see us as a single whole; everything in me is representative of the whole me, but exists in a system of inner kinships. Inside, we're a multitude of different parts with different jobs to do, different positions to hold, different responsibilities towards their fellows. And most of these parts are so very young and often terribly alone. It's all about slowly allowing that inner adult, which might be called the Self, to become strong and come to the fore, so that this essential part of us can familiarise itself with and accommodate or liberate our child parts of everything they struggle and toil with, everything they look after and are afraid of – so that these parts at last can start doing the things they want to. Feeling joy, for instance. Dancing. Laughing. Tramping contentedly along a forest path with a chainsaw in hand.

So this is what I'm doing when I lie down on the floor to be constructive with myself. And then there's everything else that goes on and happens to us in our lives. Things we can't lie down on the floor and conjur forth (I think, though, that it's all connected – albeit in deeper, more unfathomable ways – the world inside us and what happens on the outside) – a car breaking down on the road below the house on the very night, that warm spring night, when their parents have gone away, and strangers then who come barging in. The tenderness that comes from the one who stands pale and still beside you, making something possible that wasn't before. Where does that come from? Is it happening in me or in you? Is it us both?

Everything else that goes on inside us, yes. The system of inner kinships and what happens in the world outside. Okay. But then there's writing.

What is writing? What is it Vesaas does when he writes *Spring Night* into existence, allowing us to read it now, sixty-six years on, and to *be there*?

Because art isn't therapy. Therapy, when it works, can be marvellous. But art is something else. Art isn't necessarily marvellous. But art is all its own. Art can open up a very particular place all its own. A place we can't access in any other way than through art. Through a piece of writing such as *Spring Night*. *Spring Night* exists only in, only as, *Spring Night*. *Spring Night* can *happen in us* when we read it. It's not therapy, it's being. Something can happen in us, and happen *to* us, in that place. Something can reach us, and I think that what can happen there is bigger than us and has to do with the Divine, something quite simple and godlike, the sudden bright blue sky; perhaps it's all, at the same time, something that *can* open out and wash forth, inside and between us? Perhaps without our even knowing, without our feeling, the way summer comes; and when morning arives, when the car has driven on, the way the lilies of the valley open out behind the house somewhere, in the shade of some birches, a place no one knows or sees, but the fact that the lilies of the valley open out there nonetheless, and exist.

But I don't want this to end here. Because that's the way Ali Smith ends her quartet, with something growing against all odds, striving upwards, opening out into bloom. In spite of everything. Regardless. I can't do that, not when she does it, not in the same way. I don't want to be her, I want to be *unique*. The question: How to find the strength to write, the strength to confront myself with my own writing, the fact that this became *this*? How easy it is to think: Why write, when Ali Smith, when Tarjei Vesaas – ? And yet, and yet to muster that strength, to confront oneself with all the potential shame, the risk of *the mediocre*. At the same time: What's the choice? ('But who would we be if we did not try?').

I think about what I've written here about not having *allowed myself to become immersed* in the moment of death. He was here, and then he was gone. I haven't allowed myself to feel it. And if I try to go into that, as I lie meditating on the floor, it doesn't help.

But the other day I woke up from a dream: I was in a house I understood I had to leave. I had to empty the house of everything. I had to shove my bed, a single bed, aside, because underneath it was a trapdoor leading into the cellar. All the books were down there, and a fridge. I took all the books back up the stairs with me, and all the food, including what was in the freezer compartment, I took everything outside knowing I had to scatter it all about, that it all had to be strewn across the ground and left there to *decay*.

I was so devastated when I woke up. I understood that it was a dream about Luigi and me, and it opened up the grief inside me, allowing me to feel it again, so I could cry.

But when I told a friend about the dream, he said it was partly a dream of hope too. I hadn't thought about it like that, but I saw that it was that as well, in its images. The books and the food all over the place, that would fade and become obliterated, consumed, decomposing and dying away. But also the fact that it's the only way for something new to grow, it's how spring comes. And that spring is mine. If I can write that here, then that spring is yours too. If you want. It's everyone's.

ZANG DI
FOUR POEMS

Translated by Eleanor Goodman

Zang Di was born in 1964 in Beijing, and is the celebrated author of many books of poetry, including *The Simplest Human Movements Primer*, *Emotional Education Primer*, *The Association of Boiling* and *The Loquat Boy: Elegies*. He has been featured at international festivals including the Rotterdam Poetry Festival and the Princeton Poetry Festival, and has received numerous awards for both his poetry and his poetry criticism. He has been named one of China's 'Ten Most Outstanding Poets' on three separate occasions, and is a professor in the Chinese Department at Peking University.

Eleanor Goodman is the author of the poetry collection *Nine Dragon Island*, and the translator of the award-winning books *Something Crosses My Mind: Selected Poems of Wang Xiaoni*, *Iron Moon: An Anthology of Chinese Worker Poetry*, *The Roots of Wisdom: Poems by Zang Di* and *Days When I Hide My Corpse in a Cardboard Box: Poems of Natalia Chan*. She is a Research Associate at the Harvard University Fairbank Center and the recipient of a National Endowment for the Arts Translation Fellowship. Her translation of Zheng Xiaoqiong's *In the Roar of the Machine* was published by Giramondo in July.

A Step Closer than the Heart Primer

The best consolation is
I can be certain that during your life
I didn't underestimate your age.
This is the only hand the universe deals,
and there is no kind of time
that just by passing
can repair the string of a life
abruptly snapped. Beyond your shadow,
I have no other cards to play;
and if I were to try
to use the power of time to lessen
this grief of griefs, I would only be unworthy
of that dependence, stubborn in its purity,
you once had on me. Between you and me,
no other kind of trust
could fall quieter than mysteries:
in the yard, the persimmon tree we planted
is still so green it seems a parasol memorial.
I'm not startled when my vision
suddenly joins with your vision:
this unending grief is also
one fruit of life, and the difference between it
and this ashen fruit on the branch
is not so large that I can't judge it—
a pause in the thunderstorm, the sharp trill of cicadas
are life's wounds, they are memory's coarse salt.

Wintersweet on the Tip of the Nose

After your arrival, many things
once concealed behind the world
began to manifest as links
between you and me. The earliest link
seems to have been southern wintersweet
forming a little knot in early spring memory.
I encouraged you to touch the tip of your nose
to its chilly fragrance, but you had a different preference,
and stuck out your little hand to pat the remaining snow on its
    branches.
The universe won't turn gentle because of any link,
but if I remember correctly, stretch it a bit
and it turns out that tiny itch contributed to life
so many beginnings. Differentiate a bit,
intangibly, and treacherous fate
pierces a father's duty.
Tangibly, secrecy helps me keep a low profile
amid the hope of existence, converting trivial labour
into something more proper than joy.
Feed a father's pride a little,
since aside from the possibility of reincarnation
in your growth, I know
in this life, I have no other secrets.
The cradle with its fresh pad
was once a lightly swaying link; revealed
in your smile was a blossoming link;
even while you slept soundly, if I wished it,
the August moonlight was also a glimmering link.

Anything before me that tried to compete with you
lost to the name of father.
Now, the one competing is death—
its hints are formidable, it's overbearing,
it hints at time, it's already surpassed what was before,
and become the link between you and me.
But I know we still have another link
so mysterious that this true grief
is but its tiny border.

The Light of Youth Primer

Thin, but so full of energy
that even those things lit by sea waves
were unrecognisable to the waves.
A small banner of life brandished about,
a rare flash in the blue sea breeze;
more distinct, cheerful shouts burnished
the joyful jumps in the sand, until the light of youth
dazzled more than the light of life.
The final witness should never be
a father, unless rage can distil pain.
A secret so remote it seems only I can bear
its whole weight: the significance of the world
might not be supplied by you alone,
but it was extracted by you alone.
But the essence of life is heartless,
as right now, forgiveness turns me so weak
over your love that I can only identify
one bizarre scene: less than ten metres
away from me, and separated
by a big transparent pane of glass, death
snatched away the significance you brought to the world.
And so, even if I could forgive my blamelessness,
it would only betray the innocent joy you once had.

Tearful Eyes Lift Me to the Heights of Autumn Primer

At the edges of the plains, this September dawn
is like a flag at half-mast, level
against the teeming birdcalls. The corners of the eaves
look like big drill bits
abruptly abandoned by the darkness of life;
What if I were to say that insomnia is insomnia's loophole,
would you return and amid a father's love
find that single exit?
Weak, but with that nameless
bitterness, tearful eyes lift me
into the heights of autumn. Quite a climb,
and a father who's just lost his son
hasn't the strength to rely solely on attachment
to climb so high. Quite a view,
as though in our closeness,
what we felt was only some kind of cosmic effect.
When more remote than pain, life is like
a draped curtain, slowly moving in the morning light.
My son, in the blurry distance, you can't be
my personal goal. My arms still hold
an invisible weight, and it makes the nameless grief
so concrete I turn more wrathful than God.
And only a nameless wrath can scrub away
this new shame: losing you is like
mysteriously losing some kind of standing.

OSCAR SCHWARTZ
FATHER FIGURES

Oscar Schwartz is a writer and journalist. His debut collection, *The Honeymoon Stage*, was shortlisted for the 2018 Queensland Literary Award for Poetry. He lives in Melbourne.

One

I arrive at the doctor's office early in the morning. I have forgotten my mask and ask for one at the front desk. Then I take a seat in the waiting room, which looks like a professionally managed Airbnb. Exposed light bulbs and plastic ivy hang from the roof. There is a pink neon sign on the wall that says, in cursive, 'better together'.

The doctor, who wears blue chinos, a checkered shirt and R.M. Williams, calls me into his office.

'And why are we here this morning,' he asks without making eye contact. I tell him that I have been experiencing chest pain.

'I see, I see,' he says tapping notes into his computer. I haven't eaten breakfast. I feel anxious and I my fingertips go cold. I begin to take deep breaths through my nose. He takes my blood pressure and my pulse.

'Are you an athlete?' he asks. I shake my head.

'Your pulse is unusually slow,' he says, and then takes my wrist to check a second time.

'Your heart is beating thirty-seven times a minute,' he says. 'That's very slow. I'd like you have some blood tests. And an ECG, too.'

He prints off some papers and sends me back to the front desk. They have a nurse who can do the tests on site at the clinic.

'She is available now if that works for you,' says the reception-ist pointing towards a door.

Inside the door I am greeted by a woman wearing blue scrubs with straight hair cut into a bob. She tells me that she needs to take five vials of blood.

'Are you a fainter?' she asks. 'My son is a fainter, and you look just like him.'

I tell her that yes, I sometimes faint after injections.

'Well, you better lie down on the bed then. I don't think I'll be able to pick you up off the ground.'

She takes the blood. I don't faint.

She asks me to remove my top. She takes out a razor and begins to shave some hair on my chest so she can affix the electrodes for my ECG. Her hands are trembling, and she makes a small cut in my skin. She apologises repeatedly and says that she is exhausted. She has just moved back to Melbourne after thirty years living in Edinburgh. She moved there in her twenties to be with a man, a surgeon, with whom she raised two children, her son the fainter and a daughter.

'Towards the end of last year, he told me that he had fallen in love with a colleague and that he wanted a divorce. So, I said fine but then I'm moving back to Melbourne. And here I am, away from my children for the first time,' she says while dabbing the small cut on my chest with disinfectant. 'That probably doesn't mean much to someone who doesn't have children. Oh, well, isn't that presumptuous of me. I just assumed you don't have children. But do you?'

I say no, but that in the next year, maybe.

'We're talking about it,' I say.

She nods solemnly and is quiet for a moment. She tells me that her husband used to say that the pinnacle of life is when we are just an idea in our parents' mind, or a desire in their hearts, but when the embryo is formed that moment of perfection ends and decay begins.

'It is a fairly bleak way to look at it, don't you think?' she says. 'But also beautiful in its own way.'

Two

We start singing happy birthday but the person whose birthday it is doesn't hear us. He is turning ninety-one and his hearing aids have malfunctioned. He continues to eat pizza until his wife taps him on the shoulder, at which point he smiles, blows out the candles, and then continues eating his pizza.

Afterwards I am standing in a corner of the dining room eating a piece of cake. An elegant woman wearing a long, pleated skirt and conspicuous diamond earrings approaches me and wishes me 'mazal tov'.

'When I was pregnant with my first, Jack was accepted into Yale to do his PhD,' she says, placing her hand on my forearm. 'He left eight weeks before I was due. He wasn't even here for the bris. Would you believe it? You couldn't do that now.' I smile and nod.

When the baby was six weeks old, the woman continues, she got on a plane with her mother-in-law and went to join her husband in New Haven, Conneticut. They lived on the top floor of a four story walk up near the university.

'What year was this?' I ask. She says 1967.

'Must have been an interesting time to be living in New Haven,' I say.

'It was awful,' she says. 'I remember one day I took the baby to a department store to buy a toaster. A race riot broke out and we were locked inside for four hours. Of course, we had no phones back then so I couldn't get on to Jack – not that he was overly concerned. The baby cried the whole time and so did I.'

Three

I try to make eye contact with him, but he averts his gaze, so I sit down on the floor cross-legged. He slinks towards me and sits in my lap. He licks me gently a couple of times and then, without warning, bites down into the webbing between my thumb and forefinger.

It is not the first time this has happened. Just the other night, as I was watching a hot-dog-eating competition on YouTube, he leapt onto the couch and dug his fangs into my ankle. I had to pull his clamped jaw off with such force that I could hear his breathing become squeaky and asphyxiated under the pressure of my hand.

At times like this I remind myself that his violent behavior is likely a response to a traumatic infancy. The woman we adopted him from said that he and his five brothers were abandoned by their mother at two weeks of age. When kittens don't spend at least eight weeks with their mother they often develop odd social behaviours. They may be excessively shy and reserved. They may develop an obsessive and anxious relationship to food. Or as is the case with Pico, they can confuse feelings of love with feelings of aggression.

I gently massage his jaw until he releases my hand. He becomes calm and affectionate, nuzzling back into my lap and purring. I want to stay where I am and hold him. But I recently read on a forum that it is good to take some space after an attack.

I move him off me, stand and walk over to the bookshelf. He follows me and rubs his face on my legs. I take down a book that I have been reading about the mother–infant relationship in the first year of life. The author, a man, says that all a baby needs to thrive during this first stage of life is to be held properly by a mother. The ability to hold, he says, cannot be taught. There is no school for it, no books that can offer a step-by-step guide.

Holding is something each mother knows how to do instinctively for their particular child if they can just learn to trust themselves and attune to their baby.

This sounds simple enough, comforting even. But the author warns that if the mother fails to complete this one requirement the baby will suffer 'the primitive agonies', a terrifying list that includes such psychic anguish as going to pieces, falling forever, dying and dying and dying, losing all vestige of the hope of the renewal of contacts.

Four

I am drunk and riding my bike home along Canning Street. I see a man standing naked in the window of a two-storey terrace. Or at least I think that's what I see.

The fleeting image leads me to recall a poem I once read by William Carlos Williams, though I can't remember the name or any of the lines in the poem.

I pull over and search 'man naked in window poem william carlos williams'. The first result is a poem called Danse Russe. The speaker of the poem, likely Williams's avatar, recounts being in his house at night-time after his wife and baby are asleep, finally alone to do as he pleases. He is dancing naked in front of the mirror, waving his shirt around his head, singing softly:

'I am lonely, lonely.
I was born to be lonely,
I am best so!'

Five

On Twitter a guy who posts regularly about avant-garde poetry, machine learning, and David Bowie says having a baby

53

seems bad to him because it reorients adult life back towards childhood and childhood is an awful time, so awful that most adults have wilfully forgotten it, an amnesia that allows them to now selfishly have children to satisfy their egos or fill an existential void.

A surprising number of people agree in comments: yes, they say, childhood is filled with shame and fear, and starting a family reproduces this suffering.

One man disagrees. He says that having children is like romantic love – an experience both painful and beautiful. And just like with love, for some reason the suffering is easy to talk about. But when you try to describe the beauty, it just ends up sounding like self-justifying propaganda.

Six

'I am so stressed about the whole thing that I think I gave myself heart irregularities,' I tell my friend. 'I have to see a cardiologist.'

We are bobbing in the water at St Kilda Beach, watching the sun set. He laughs and then tells me that his parents are getting divorced after more than fifty years of marriage.

'They met at high school,' he says. 'I don't think they have ever had sex with anyone else but each other.'

He went to visit his dad a week earlier in his new apartment in the city. They were supposed to go out for breakfast, but instead his dad took a packet of Golden Gaytimes out of the freezer and said they could eat ice cream for breakfast.

'And I sat there at this long trestle table watching him eat his ice cream in a really strange way. He kept turning the ice cream on its side and, like, biting at it, like he couldn't even figure out how to eat an ice cream now.'

The sun sets into the ocean and everyone at the beach spontaneously applauds. We get out of the sea and eat fish and chips. Then we walk back along the Esplanade to his apartment. Around a bend in the path, we see strange fluorescent figures on the rocks leading down to the ocean. As we get closer, we see that they are fisherman wearing helmets to which they have fixed brightly coloured LED lights.

My friend tells me that the fishermen look like a species of grasshopper aliens he once encountered during a DMT trip. 'They descended from the sky and asked me if I wanted a full body scan and I just politely said no thanks,' he says. 'It was very empowering.'

Later, outside his apartment, as we are saying goodbye, he tells me to wait a minute and races inside. He returns holding a brass film canister.

'There is some DMT in here if you want,' he says handing the canister over. 'It might help you come to terms with things.'

Seven

I am getting dressed in front of the cardiologist in his corner office with floor-to-ceiling windows overlooking Fitzroy Gardens. He has just completed several tests on my heart and lungs.

'Your heart isn't only healthy, it is exceptionally healthy,' he says. 'Are you under any particular stress at the moment?' The doctor is in great shape, with luscious grey hair parted in the middle and swept back behind his ears, like Paul McCartney I think. On his desk there around a dozen photographs of him with his family – a wife and four sons. They are on a beach, playing tennis, toasting each other with champagne, at a wedding, a skiing vacation.

I surprise myself by telling him that I am expecting my first child in the middle of the year. He smiles broadly and clasps his hands together. He tells me that being a father is 'a slog' but what 'makes it all worth it' is when you 'see your son doing something that a good person does', like sharing or 'being a good loser'.

Eight

My flight to Darwin is delayed due to bad weather. At the departure gate a mother is playing a game of air cricket with her son to pass the time. She takes a theatrically long run up. He stands waiting, imaginary bat in hand, wearing a black tracksuit and white Air Jordans.

'Go on,' he shouts.

She sprints towards him and releases the imaginary ball. He swings.

'Catch it,' a man wearing a cowboy hat, also waiting for the delayed flight, shouts.

The mother follows the non-existent ball up into the air and begins to run backwards. Everyone is watching.

'Catch it,' the cowboy shouts again.

The mother leaps into the air with her right arm extended, closing her hand into a fist.

'Got him!' the cowboy shouts. 'You're out, son.'

Nine

It is election day, and we are at a birthing course in a church hall. The facilitator, a charismatic woman with curly red hair and prominent cheekbones, stands in front of around a dozen pregnant women and their exclusively male partners.

'Do we have any willing women here today?' she begins. A few women reluctantly raise their hands and look around.

'That wasn't very resounding,' the facilitator says. 'And I don't blame you.'

A willing woman, she explains, is one who is willing to have a 'normal physiological childbirth', which means birthing through the vagina with no intervention – no pain killers, no forceps, no epidurals. There are not many willing women anymore but this is not women's fault. Modern obstetrics is designed to make women afraid of 'normal physiological childbirth'. Pain is characterized as dangerous and evil, something that can be entirely managed by the well-trained (historically male) obstetrician.

'I'm not saying that all men are bad, but it is important to recognise that their role in childbirth is problematic at a population level,' she says. 'They make things harder by trying to take control of our pain. But what is labour pain?'

The facilitator pauses theatrically and then proceeds to explain that it is feminine creative power expressing itself and that men do not want to see women in pain because it generates fear. We might think this fear is protective and superficially maybe it is. But at a deeper, instinctive level men are afraid of this pain because it is beyond their control.

In traditional societies, she continues, men were not allowed to be around during labour. They were expected to go out hunting, collect food, and protect the space around the birthing area. 'Even the father's flat, low vocal tone can make the baby feel threatened, as if there is predator around,' she says.

I look around at the other men in the room, who are mostly dressed in Uniqlo and appear to be in a state of extreme passivity, apart from one man with a shaved head and a beard who is nodding attentively. My eyes linger on him. There is something odd about the way he blinks, like each blink is consciously premeditated.

I notice that he also compulsively massages his wife's shoulders. She has extremely long red hair and has now taken a seat on one of the pillows on the floor, leaning back into his knees. When morning tea time comes all the other couples line up to make themselves coffee and select a snack, except for this couple. They stay seated on the floor, eye-gazing. Then he starts doing a series of yoga moves culminating in a head stand.

'Impressive,' the facilitator says.

Ten

We're at a gallery, the opening of a friend's new show, standing in front of a sculpture that looks like a cage made from baguettes. The artist's partner explains that the sculpture is in fact made of hundreds of baguettes that have been coated in a glass resin and held together with sticks of wood.

'We call it the Bread Prison,' he says.

I walk to the bar and order a soda water and gin and tonic. The bartender, who has a neat mullet, tells me that his partner is also pregnant, and pours me a double shot of gin.

'Drinking for three now, legend,' he says.

Eleven

On my way into the pasta shop I see an old friend.

'How long until the baby now?' he asks.

In tell him around six weeks while craning my head to see what type of pasta is in the bain-marie today. Gnocchi Napoli.

Some sort of pasta bake. Cheese ravioli in bacon and cream sauce.

I order the gnocchi and the woman who serves me, the daughter of the woman who owns the shop, says: 'I didn't mean to stickybeak, but did I hear you're having a baby?' I nod.

'Oh, that's amazing,' she says. 'Oh, how lovely. Girl or boy?'

'We decided not to find out,' I say, taking a seat at the counter.

'I'd need to know because me and mum crochet, so I'd have to know what colour to make the blankets,' she says passing me three slices of buttered bread. 'And just so you know girls rule. I had a friend whose first was a girl and he wanted a boy for his second and when it was a girl, he called me up and said, "Now who am I going to take to the footy?"'

I say that I grew up in a family with three sisters, so I think I'd be comfortable either way. She says she also grew up in a family with three girls and one boy, but that it was more like being in a family with three boys and one girl.

'Don't ask me to elaborate,' she says.

'Do you have any kids?' I ask.

'Oh no, not me,' she says. 'I told mum if I haven't met the right person by thirty-five, I'll do it alone. Honestly it would probably be easier doing it without a man anyway. I'm seeing someone right now. He has three daughters so I can see what he'd be like as a father.'

'And?' I ask.

She does the so-so gesture with her hand.

Twelve

John from Wodonga is topless and has a ring in each nipple. He is wearing a 2XU hat. He has broad shoulders, a short beard, and braces. He is feeding a his seven-month-old son a bottle.

I am interviewing John for a magazine article (which I won't get around to writing) about men who become fathers on their own via surrogacy. This has only become a legal possibility in Australia recently, John says, and to his knowledge, he is the first to do it.

Over the past hour John has told me the story – how he found himself at age thirty-three single and desperate for a biological child; how he found an egg donor; how his sister-in-law, who already had four children, offered to be his surrogate; and how when his son was delivered, the umbilical cord was cut, the baby was placed immediately on John's chest, and the surrogate, his sister-in-law, was swiftly taken out of the room.

The baby has now become restless and begins to whine. As John puts him over his shoulder to burp, the baby vomits all over his chest. John sighs dramatically.

'Things change when you become a mum,' he says.

'You see yourself as his mum?' I ask.

John says that in the weeks after his son was born, he felt his body begin to change, as if were preparing him for lactation. 'My body fat grew. I got man boobs. My testosterone levels just plummeted. Where I could lift a hundred and eighty kilos before, now I struggle with a hundred. I've been known to be quite horny, too, one of the horniest people you've ever met. My sex drive pretty much went to zero overnight.'

With these physical changes came a realisation that a mother does not have to be a woman. The mother is simply the primary nurturing figure in the baby's life. 'I care, I feed, I get up at night, I change the nappies,' he says. 'I do all that for him. That's what makes me his mum.'

The baby has now settled and is nuzzling into John's chest. 'The person I was before has died. I have grieved that person. I loved that person. I didn't think it would change me this much,' he says. 'But that person has gone and here I am. When the baby was born, I was born.'

Thirteen

I am in a workshop facilitated by a writer who wrote a book about working through her ambivalence concerning motherhood. I always remember one part of this book where she says that if, as a girl, no one had ever told her anything about the adult world she likely would have invented, boyfriends, sex, friendship and art. She would not have invented child rearing.

As far as I can tell, through my screen, the writer is in some sort of country house. There is a window and outside I can see what looks like the countryside in summer, in Italy or something. But I might be imagining this, or projecting. It is two-thirty a.m. where I am. It is cold and the middle of winter. I am on the couch, having taken 5 mg of dexamphetamine to stay awake for this workshop, aware that soon I'll no longer be able to do things like this anymore.

The workshop is odd, funny, unstructured, and chaotic, much like the writer's books. She talks and gives pieces of wisdom in koān-like sentences.

'Plot exists in the reader not writer.'

'A working title is a container.'

'Don't be careful with your draft. Kill it and let it come back to life.'

The message she comes back to repeatedly, though, is that writing is mostly painful, so you must find what is pleasurable

61

in it and then follow the pleasure, to make sure you keep writing.

'It is like having kids,' she says. 'Not that it's something I've done. But apparently you forget the pain and just remember the high. That's why people do it again.'

Fourteen

After cleaning the house, I drive to a friend's place to pick up an oil heater. The baby will be born in the middle of winter and we need a way of keeping the room warm.

We drink a beer and she asks how I am. I say I feel like I'm in limbo, like before going on a long trip or moving cities.

'I know that things are going to change soon and I'm kind of just waiting for the change,' I say.

She says her sister met a man and six months later they had a baby and are now expecting another. 'It feels like they're new people,' she says. 'Like she's lost herself.'

'That's what scares me,' I say.

She nods. 'But there are people who do it their own way,' she says, and asks if I know Sally and Marie. I don't.

'Because they had their first child just recently and I still see them out all the time,' she says. 'But they're poly so I guess they're used to being flexible.'

Fifteen

I am driving past a KFC when out of nowhere I remember an ancient Egyptian proverb. 'We all die twice. First when we stop breathing and then again, a bit later on, the last time someone says our name.'

Around ten minutes later I pull into the Baby Bunting car

park and look up the proverb on my phone. On a forum, a person called 'moose_man' says that the proverb is not in fact Egyptian but was first spoken by the anonymous street artist, Banksy. Another person called 'HurricaneDNA' disagrees: 'I believe it was actually David Eagleman who said this first.' I type 'David Eagleman' into Google but before I can read the results someone knocks on my window.

He asks me if my name is Oscar. I say yes. He tells me he has been waiting for me and asks me to get out of the car.

'Have you installed a bub seat before?' he asks. I say I haven't. I am paying him money to install a baby seat safely, as recommended by the retailer. He is wearing a red polo shirt with a badge on it that says: 'Baby on Board'. His hair is pulled back in a tight bun. It looks like he has shaved his widow's peak to make his hairline straight, but the widow's peak is beginning to grow back, leaving a patch of triangle-shaped stubble on his forehead. He is grinning and not making eye contact.

It takes him five minutes to install the seat and after he is done, I ask him to show me how to strap the baby in safely.

'Where's the baby?' he asks, turning his head around both ways dramatically like the baby was somewhere nearby and had escaped.

'It isn't here yet,' I say.

'Of course,' he says. 'It isn't here yet.'

He shows me how to strap the baby into the car seat and then says that we can pretend that his arm is the baby, to practice. I carefully take hold of his white, hairless forearm and place it in the baby seat and strap it in. He begins wriggling his fingers. 'This is where the legs go and they will really wriggle like this,' he says. 'Like tiny frog legs.'

Days later, when I show Jess how to use the baby seat, I can still see the fingers wriggling where the real legs will shortly go. I think about the wisdom of Banksy but inverted. If we die twice how many times are we born?

KENNY PITTOCK
POST-IT NOTES FOUND WHILE
WORKING IN A SUPERMARKET

Kenny Pittock is an artist based in Naarm/Melbourne. Since graduating from the Victorian College of the Arts in 2013, he has held solo exhibitions in Italy, Singapore and New Zealand, and exhibited throughout Australia including at ACCA, PICA, Artspace in Sydney and MONA. Pittock's work is represented in many public collections including Artbank, Deakin University, Monash University, University of Queensland, and the City of Melbourne Art and Heritage Collection.

These ceramic recreations of post-it notes are from the series *Twenty-Four Shopping Lists Written on Post-It Notes Found While Working in a Supermarket,* which was exhibited at Olsen Annexe in 2022.

Images pp. 67–72
Kenny Pittock
Something for Dinner – Macaroni Maybe?; *Eggs to Boil*; *10 Kebabs*; *Wine*; *Gargle – Whitening*; *Dog Food My Dog*
acrylic on ceramic
7.7 × 7.7 cm
courtesy of the artist

Something for dinner
— macaroni maybe?

- bacon
- spring onion
- macaroni pack
_____

bread
iced coffees
toilet roll

pesto
chicken
cheese
zucchini
carrot
sweet potato
brocoli
cordial
eggs to boil

3 x Soulaki Bread
10   Kebabs
  1   Avocado
  4   Tomatoes
  1   lettuce
  1   Tazik!

Nachoss

Corn
  — Chips

  — tasty cheese

  — sauce

  — avocado
    (wine)

Strawberries

Peanut butter-Crunchy
corn
~~Oats~~ – Plain
Baked beans
Green/red capcicum
~~Red onion~~
Sweet potato
Muesli boxs
white rice
cucumber
~~baby~~ tomatos
Mix salad
pumpkin

Gargle — whitening

Pads (pink)

milk.
weetbix
yoghurt.
dog food my dog
toilet paper.
sardines

AMITAVA KUMAR
DEAR EDITOR

Amitava Kumar is a writer and
journalist. He was born in Ara, India,
and grew up in the nearby town of
Patna, famous for its corruption,
crushing poverty and delicious
mangoes. Kumar is the author of
the novels *Immigrant, Montana* and
A Time Outside This Time, as well as
several other books of non-fiction
and fiction. He lives in Poughkeepsie,
New York, where he is Professor of
English and the Helen D. Lockwood
Chair at Vassar College.

DEAR EDITOR, *both bathrooms at the back of the Air India flight from New York to Mumbai were out of order. The doors had* Not Working *stickers pasted over their metal handles. Identical stickers, from different days, stuck on top of earlier ones.*

In the op-ed that I had already begun to compose in my head, I was going to write that the bathroom doors were *festooned* with yellow stickers.

The plane hadn't taken off yet from JFK. I needed to use the bathroom. But what I'm trying to tell you is that I felt I was already home.

Excuse me, I said to a passing flight attendant. These bathrooms can't be used?

The woman was Indian, and I guessed Punjabi. She slowed down momentarily. With a show of patience that barely masked her contempt, she gave a tight smile and asked, Did you see the sticker?

I did, I said. And then, raising my voice, But the stickers look so old, so many of them, I wasn't sure if there was one also from today.

She retained her smile, pretending that she had not heard me, and said that there were bathrooms in the front of the cabin.

What I really wanted her to confirm was that the bathrooms at the back hadn't worked for many days. I wondered whether fresh – except *fresh* was the wrong word in this context – stickers were slapped on the doors before the plane took flight each day. Honesty is a more bracing ingredient than bad faith in a story, and I wanted the Air India staff to give me a candid account of what it was that I was witnessing. I got up from my seat but before wandering to the bathroom in the front I went back to the locked bathrooms and took pictures of the stickers on my phone.

My ability to exaggerate does on occasion get the better of me but, believe me, I'm not being fanciful when I say that even the blue carpet in the aisles exuded a faecal odour – no, a heavier element, a moist miasma, that entered the nose and seemed to paralyse the senses. This preceding sentence was going into the op-ed. Also this one: I had a ringing headache by the time we took off.

The flight attendants, betraying a suspicious expertise in the situation, walked down the aisle with the nozzles of air fresheners aimed only inches from the floor. I didn't move in my seat, convinced that ordure was stuck to my shoes. From my breast pocket I extracted my notebook and wrote down what I was seeing and feeling, as if the tiny page that fitted into my palm was a window I could open. My neighbour in the next seat, a businessman from Surat, was amused by my agitation. He soothed me with the news that the previous month an Air India flight that had taken off from Mumbai for London was forced to return because a rat was racing up and down the length of the plane.

The hotel in Mumbai, where the wedding was being held, faced the sea. The lounge had impossibly high ceilings that gave the hotel's plush interior a false sense of quiet. Young women in peacock-blue and orange saris stood behind the reception counter. The large glass windows framed a view of the swallowing darkness but close by, where the land ended, there stretched an undulating, glittering necklace of white lights. The wedding guests, some of whom had travelled huge distances and were counting the number of time zones they had crossed, sat on sofas holding drinks in their hands. Two Arab men in their spotless white robes turned away from the check-in desk and regarded our group. Had they not seen all of this before? No doubt some of the gold on display on the bodies of my fellow guests had been purchased in Dubai and Abu Dhabi.

A waiter came by with a tray filled with dainty little sandwiches and then a couple of minutes later another one stopped by to offer a colourful, thoroughly exotic description of something small and elegant-looking at the end of a toothpick. The woman seated next to me was older than me by at least two decades; from her air of reserve, I guessed that she was a teacher or a bureaucrat. At her request, a waiter brought her a pot of green tea and she sipped solemnly from a delicate china cup. I, on the other hand, was in no mood to hold back on the jalapeño margaritas. After a few sips I turned to address her, even though I didn't have a joke ready, but she was looking the other way. I decided to wait.

We were in the third week of December, 2016. The thought of the unwritten op-ed returned to me in a new way. In this last month of the year, hordes of desis settled abroad return to India and you can hear the twang of stretched-out Westernised syllables in upscale restaurants, chic boutiques and colonial-era clubs. The talk is always the same. A mix of arrogance and condescension accompanied by an ability for unceasing wonder at how bad things are in some places. As it is, those who speak in English in India generally speak louder to their children, to waiters, and even to strangers, but the assault on the ears is especially painful when the face is brown and the accent is American. Despite my long years abroad, I haven't acquired the accent yet. Still, it struck me that I had become one of those I had so far been railing against.

77

I turned again to the woman sitting next to me. Was she deliberately keeping her face turned away from me?

I wished to confide in my neighbour. I wanted to say to her: Look at me. How crude, how banal, to have become that person who complains loudly about the smell of shit. Trump has just last month been elected President and if I, an Indian living in New York, make demeaning comments about India, don't you think newspaper readers in Mumbai and Delhi will judge me harshly?

I was sure that on Twitter a troll would provide a link to my op-ed and paste a picture of the White House underneath with the question: *Are you sure the smell isn't coming from there?*

As I took my second drink in hand, I saw Satish approaching with a smile. He bowed slightly in front of my neighbour and then looked inquiringly at me. I was seized by the sudden fear that he was signalling that the old woman was a teacher from our school and asking whether I had recognised her.

I looked at my neighbour again but I didn't think I had seen her before. Satish asked her if she was comfortable and then looking at me said that he was going to make an announcement and he would appreciate it if I made a short speech after he was done.

What did he want me to speak about?

You are the writer, he said. Say anything you want.

Satish and I had first met at his mother's school as eight-year-old boys. Minnie Aunty was the principal at Growing Minds in Patna. Three years before we met, his father had died. The plane in which he was travelling had crashed into the Himalayan ranges in the north-east, the fog so dense in the mountains that no search could be conducted for the next five days. But Minnie Aunty, almost single-handedly, established her school and made a life not just for herself and Satish but also for so many of us in that town.

When I rose up to speak, I took in the already bored faces of the guests, their excess finery, and it is possible I felt a bit superior, but I was also sharply conscious of my desire to engage my audience. I knew I could neither entertain nor enlighten them: these shortcomings were mine and not theirs. I said that on this occasion I missed Satish's mother whom I had known as a boy. It was impossible for me to look back at Satish's and my own childhood and not find Minnie Aunty in it: it was like imagining the earth without the grounding force of gravity. And now Satish and Ratna were seeing their daughter getting married. Our children were charting their own paths, discovering their own orbits. A new beginning, etc.

There was much that I did not mention in my speech.

When Satish and I were students at Growing Minds, Minnie Aunty would take us with her to visit every new district magistrate. She wanted to be the first to ask the officer's kids to join her school. This was her unbending policy and I was too young to know why she did this. The school enjoyed many benefits, including the advantage of having a police tent outside the main gate. All the main events enjoyed some form of government patronage. Students from our school appeared each year at the Republic Day parade and presented the governor with a bouquet of flowers. In our home, although my mother disapproved of this, my father only referred to Minnie Aunty as 'Indira Gandhi'. I had at first innocently assumed that he was simply thinking of her as a great leader. What added pathos to the comparison in my young mind was that just like the prime minister, Minnie Aunty was also a widow. When I grew older, I saw in my father's words bitter criticism of Minnie Aunty's drive to power, and then, when I was older still, I thought that perhaps my father had felt himself powerless in her company, a man without real ambition.

Time passed. Satish went away to an engineering college and then to MIT and from there to Wharton. In my case, after having toiled for years as a reporter in Delhi, I came to Georgetown to get a degree and visited Satish in New Jersey over Thanksgiving. I was seeing him after years. He picked me up in his BMW and drove me to his house, a mansion set down on eighteen acres of rolling greens in Hunterdon County. It didn't take me long to realise that we had nothing in common except for our past. Perhaps Satish understood this too, but he wasn't the type to be troubled by such thoughts. It was not in his nature. It is also possible that he had grown so enormously rich that my presence didn't register as a question in his mind. I was only a small fact in his life, someone who had known his mother, his childhood home, and the white dog he had got when he was a teenager.

He believed, and rightly so, that I had reverence for his mother even though I was certain that he had misjudged its basis. I didn't respect his mother because she had been the principal of our school, or because she was like a kind aunt to me and was now dead, but because she was forgiving. There had been that episode at school when I had hidden the Muhammad Ali autobiography under my jacket but had been stopped by the librarian. Once, I traded Satish's stamps from Norway with one that I had from Nepal of the king wearing his crown with a plume of feathers. I had claimed that the stamp I had given him was an extremely rare one, and then, as luck would have it, a letter arrived for Minnie Aunty from Kathmandu with five of the same stamps on the envelope. Or, later still, the accident with Satish's dog, Bhola, and its mangled paw.

When I look back now, there is always Minnie Aunty pointing to something good awaiting me in the future. Until she did that, I did not know what the future meant. I was fifteen, say, and sitting in the bus taking me to my grandmother's village. Beside the road, standing in the hot glare of the sun, next to a cart with shrivelled green vegetables was a dark-skinned woman. I would wonder how much she would make that day, and how selling a bit of spinach and coriander was possibly going to satisfy her needs. Such questions, for which I had no answers, were what the word *future* meant to me. The future at that age was a wide river in flood, and I didn't have a boat, and if I waded into the waters I would drown. *Dear editor, The problem isn't that the young desire to do wrong but, often, their inability to separate right from wrong. This ability arrives only with a sense of consequences, which is linked to an idea of time. The young cannot imagine a time outside their time.* After the worst, most shameful incident, Minnie Aunty came to the jail where I had already spent a week. She signed the statements for my release, and two months later, I left for college and never looked back. I thought of Minnie Aunty often, and never without a great sense of gratitude. But you can't tell all this to unknown wedding guests.

It turned out that the old woman seated next to me was Minnie Aunty's closest friend. That is how she introduced herself. She said her name was Ranjana Ghosal.

I told her that I was afraid that she had been a teacher at our school and that I hadn't recognised her. She laughed. She said she was a retired doctor.

Did she live in Mumbai now?

No, she said. I live in a small town very far from here.

I asked her the town's name. She said, You won't know the name. Khunti, it is close to Ranchi.

I gave a startled laugh. Khunti was a name from my childhood. I told her that my father had been a trainee magistrate there, living in a tiny government-owned house with my mother and sister.

Maybe it was because of the margaritas but I found myself telling the doctor that it was hard for me to imagine a similar conversation taking place with a stranger in the town where I live in America. The last wedding that I attended was in Clinton Corners in upstate New York; the groom was Chinese and the bride Italian. A beautiful event offering a lesson about how newness comes into the world. But there was nothing there to take me back to my past.

I asked Dr Ghosal if Growing Minds was still there. Had it closed down now?

No, she said, Ramesh runs it. He is doing a great job.

Ramesh!

Every middle-class home in our town had a houseboy or maid from a lower caste, who ate leftovers and slept in a corner and, during festivals or time of need, sent a bit of money back to the family. The young man at Minnie Aunty's house wore crisp, clean shirts and trousers. His name was Ramesh, and we were not allowed to call him Ramu. All of this was new to me, highly unusual and it took some getting used to because when we sat down at the dining table for meals, Ramesh always ate with us. This wasn't the situation in my house, nor was this anything

82

like I had seen in any other house. Ramesh addressed Minnie Aunty as Didi, or elder sister, and that too was new to me. Later I learned that Ramesh was attending classes at Growing Minds and, still later, that he had enrolled in Patna College.

And he was now the principal of the school!

A lesson in democracy. If I was honest, maybe this was the op-ed I would actually write.

Unbidden tears came to my eyes. I realised I was being melodramatic. The doctor noticed my eyes watering and said that she was sorry that she had made me sad. No, no, I said, I'm so moved. Believe me, I spend all year mocking the kinds of things that happen in India. I'll be at a party and someone will begin to ask something about cows, for example, and even before their question is complete, I start asking the host or hostess where is my drink, where is my glass of cow urine. It is so easy to do that sort of thing. But then you think of someone like Ramesh –

I stopped because a waiter, probably hearing me ask about my drink, had now brought me another jalapeño margarita.

Dr Ghosal asked, What do you remember of your childhood in Khunti?

My parents left Khunti when I was perhaps two. My father was transferred to Patna. I had no memories. I was hungry, I told her, to learn from her. What was Khunti like in those years?

I suspect she was free of nostalgia. She looked at me kindly and then at her watch. It is as if she was about to count my pulse. Then she began to speak.

—

You will hear many people who are sitting around us complaining that when they stepped out on the hotel's terrace they could not find a wi-fi connection. The trauma of bad connectivity in the jewellery market. That there is no HBO. Well, when I went to Khunti we were decades before the internet. Actually, there was no TV, and not even telephones for everyone. There was a telephone in the Civil Lines office. The particular distraction of watching sitcoms on TV wasn't to come until two decades later, although you could go to Ranchi to watch a movie in a theatre. But where was the time to travel for an hour or more each way on the bus? We were in the middle of hills and iron ore mines. Thick sal forests surrounded us. I didn't own a car for a long time. To make matters worse, there was famine in nearby parts, in Palamu, which gave an excuse for the government not to pay us on time. Salaries were delayed and the officials held up funds. I would have to use my own money, or borrow it, to buy what was needed in the clinic. Anything from a bar of Lifebuoy soap to purchasing penicillin for common infections. Or streptomycin for my tuberculosis patients. A life of scarcity. But there was one bit of pleasure in our lives, a nice thing to look forward to, and this was that we played badminton each evening. The subdivisional magistrate was a man in his late twenties named Kumar Raghuvansh. He was married and didn't have any children when we first met. This man and his wife Sheela were very kind to me. The badminton court was in the open, on a part of their large, three- or four-acre official compound. We played under lights with the magistrate's staff bringing us iced lemon or orange squash in the summer and milky tea with ginger and cardamom in the winter.

A young indigenous studies lecturer would come on weekends and after our badminton games we ate together. Chicken was cheaper there than in places like Patna. Fresh vegetables. We ate well. I liked this man, the Adivasi scholar, who was himself indigenous, who was good at many languages and also played the flute. His name was Ram Naresh Nag. We fell in love and got married. That was in 1971. Raghuvansh, the magistrate who had become our friend, was from a small royal family but he was committed to the people. At the time, Adivasis were displayed each year on Republic Day in Delhi as simple tribal folk with bows and arrows, the bare-chested aboriginal people who loved to sing and dance. Adivasis had educated leaders even then; we didn't know about them, we were just privileged outsiders, *dikus*. But Raghuvansh was interested in the history of rebellion among the Adivasis and he was writing a biography of Birsa Munda who had been hanged by the British. I liked to see the two of them working together. The magistrate's father had been the ruler of what was once a small principality under the British and his grandfather had attended Queen Victoria's coronation as her guest. He had gifted an elephant for the ceremony. You can see the giant, placid creature in the archival photographs of the royal event even if it is difficult to make out Raghuvansh's ancestor in the crowd. Birsa Munda was unknown to Indians at that time; now you find his portrait hanging in the halls of the Parliament in Delhi. That process of his discovery began in those years in Khunti when Raghuvansh would go into villages and examine the dusty government gazettes from decades ago to find out more about Birsa Munda and his fierce fight against the British.

During weekends, Ram Naresh and Raghuvansh would sit for hours translating songs and other texts from Mundari and Santhali to Hindi or English. At the day's end, we would sit and eat, all of us always together. Ram would charm us by playing on the flute. We drove on Sundays in Raghuvansh's ambassador car to the waterfalls nearby – Dassam, Perwaghagh, Panchghagh – all within a quick driving distance. There wasn't much traffic in the forests in those days. We would pass peacocks. All around us the noise of waterfalls. We would stop and have our picnic on the giant rocks near the falling waters.

You know, when I travel to other parts of India, or even close by to places like Patna, at least in progressive circles or among intellectuals, there will be someone who will always ask me about the recent lynchings in the area where the Adivasis live. What is happening these days, people ask. I don't know. There was violence before too. A few years before I started living there, a Catholic priest, a German, had been killed in Khunti. The priest was trying to protect a few Muslims from a Hindu mob. He said to the angry crowd that they would have to kill him before they could enter the church with their weapons. So, that is what they did. They hacked him to death right there at the threshold.

Your question was about what I remember of the past. And I don't know whether I'm answering your question. Do you want me to go on?

Yes, I replied. Please, please go on. It wasn't the alcohol, I was convinced that it was her story, her voice, warm and steady like a candle flame on a still night, that kept my attention focused on what she was telling me.

I said earlier that it took too much effort to drive all the way to Ranchi to watch a Hindi film. While that is true, we still made the trip on several occasions. When that happened, Ram would wait for us in Ranchi. Those were the years when Rajesh Khanna was the most popular actor in Bollywood. The driver and the magistrate sat in the front seat of the ambassador; Sheela and I sat at the back. Ram would meet us at the cinema hall. We always ate aloo chaat and drank Coca-Cola before the film started. Afterwards, we went to a restaurant for dinner before driving back.

Ram stayed in my flat after we got married. We had a civil ceremony. My mother wasn't opposed to my marrying an Adivasi but the rest of my family was. My two maternal uncles were angry with me. They saw the dark-skinned Adivasis and thought of them as savages. My father had died when I was young and these uncles had assumed charge. But my mother was financially independent; she taught in the school where Minnie later became the principal. Minnie came down to Ranchi when I got married. She was my witness in the magistrate's office.

Do you know what a softie is? There is a shop in Ranchi called Firayalal. It had a new machine for making softie ice cream. Ram, his friend Subhas, who was a teacher in Saraikela, and Minnie and I went on two rickshaws to Firayalal to have softies after we got out of the magistrate's office. You wanted to know about the past. Well, there you have a little glimpse of what weddings were like in those days. We didn't have the money to meet like this in five-star hotels.

The war with Pakistan happened, the war that led to the liberation of Bangladesh. I was asked to report to the army camp nearby where Pakistani prisoners of war were kept. It was winter. The prisoners were disciplined and I had to do a quick medical examination to determine whether or not they needed treatment. Most of them only wanted to be able to make the announcement on radio that they were alive and well. The radio announcement was broadcast also from a loudspeaker on top of a pole in the field where the prisoners sat in the sun. The prisoners heard their own voices from the loudspeaker – name, father's name, name of village or town, regimental identification, and a short message about health and wellbeing – but I couldn't understand how the announcement was also reaching the families in Pakistan. Raghuvansh, the magistrate, assured me that it was.

—

The doctor had stopped speaking. A waiter in a maroon jacket had come to us to say that the party was moving outside to the pool. The two of us got up from our sofa. Despite her age, the doctor held herself erect as she walked ahead of me. Her hair was gathered in a small bun. I wondered what she was thinking. I had only just met her but I was taken with her. I was unaware just how this transition had happened but mentally I had put her among the old women from Bhopal that, during an earlier visit, I had seen protesting outside the Supreme Court in Delhi. They wanted justice from Union Carbide. There had been no clean-up even though three decades had passed since the gas leak; new generations of children were still being born with deformed limbs. These old women seemed to have their own mind, their own strength, they were not owned by any party or political group; they had taken what life had thrown at them, over many decades, and they had hoarded their tribulations, and used this startling inventory of defeats and small triumphs to remind themselves and others that they were survivors. Nothing would move them, and they wanted answers. At the back of their minds, maybe there was also the thought that it could not be long before they would be dead and soon forgotten. And so, they were afraid of nothing. *Dear editor, Most of the names on your masthead belong to men, and although I spot a smattering of women, do you have any older than sixty? Recently I met a woman in Mumbai, a retired doctor, who told me...*

When we stepped out, I saw that a raised platform, decorated with flowers, was in place at the near end of the pool. Drinks were being served by a bartender standing under a festive umbrella bedecked with ornate flowers made entirely of sequins. We walked over to the chairs at the other end of the pool. White lights glowed underwater while the breeze ruffled the pool's surface as if it were fur on an animal's back.

What have you been drinking? I think I'll have one too.

The doctor took a sip of her jalapeño margarita. She smiled and nodded, and then looked around.

Tell me, she said, because you have lived both here and abroad. Do you think that because weddings in India take so long to complete – do you think that is the reason why marriages last here so long too? In the West people probably get married in an hour and then divorced in a week. Or that is what many of us believe here.

I laughed with her. And then she calmly, unaffectedly, went on with her story.

—

Soon after I got married to Ram, she said, a government order informed me that I had been transferred to Dhanbad. I didn't want to go. I had established myself in Khunti. The town was changing, growing fast, and I thought I was needed there anyway. I resigned from my government job and started my own practice in a rented room next to a machine parts and hardware store. Instead of calling the clinic Nursing Medical Home, Ram wanted me to call it Narsing Medical Home. Narsing is a Munda name popular among the Adivasis – it was also the name that had belonged to Ram's father. Ram was playful that way. He said that just because of the name my clinic would be liked among his people. I accepted his suggestion.

My assistant at the government clinic agreed to work for me part-time, she continued. His job was to come in the evenings and serve as dispenser of medicines and blood tests. He was from Deoghar and his name was Adishankar. His wife had died recently and he had a little daughter. She came to the clinic with him and kept us amused, dancing the little filmi numbers, her hips moving this way and that. Adishankar was an efficient man, good at administering injections or swabs but also handy with tools. The table fan is making a ticking noise? Let Adishankar take a look! There is a water leak? Wait for Adishankar. If I rented a car, for myself or a patient, Adishankar was there as a driver. He had of course never owned a car, and he had never been employed as a driver before. Where had he learned to drive? I asked him but he just smiled.

I also had a female nurse, who was Adivasi like Ram, and also like him a Christian convert. She has remained with me all these years, a small, hard-working woman, ten or twelve years younger than me. Her name was Maryam. Over the years, I began to think of her as my shadow. So many times, when I was delivering a baby, or performing a minor surgery, I felt that she knew already what I was going to do next.

The story I want to tell you is about change, and the first inkling I got of it came from Maryam. She told me one morning that she had eaten a heavy meal the previous day. This was most probably in August or September in 1990. I remember that Rajiv Gandhi was the prime minister. He hadn't been killed in that bomb blast yet. I asked Maryam to tell me about the occasion for the feast. She said that her brother Peter had become a Hindu at a ceremony organised by his employer. Everyone had been fed. There was a feast with rice, dal, two different vegetables. For dessert, sweet jalebis. A priest had done a puja. Peter had been given a new name. His name was now Ramsewak. Maryam began to laugh. She said that Peter's employer, Anil Sharma, had washed Peter's feet before the puja. The washing of the feet signified that after a long journey Peter had returned home: he wasn't a Christian anymore and was back to being a Hindu. It could be argued that the Adivasis had never really been Hindus, but politicians like Sharma had their theories.

Peter now had three names. The name that the padre called him and which was on his ration card; the new name that the *diku* Sharma gave him; and his oldest name, his tribal name, Donka, that he had from his childhood. Maryam thought it was funny that all the four men who were converted were Anil Sharma's employees. Peter drove one of the two buses that Sharma owned; another, an Oraon man, was the cleaner on the other bus; and two others worked in Sharma's grocery store, Mata Top Quality Kirana.

Long before Peter started working for him, Anil Sharma had come to my clinic. By the town's standards he was a prosperous man, but he had a rough look. His family owned a gas station in Jamshedpur, and his older brother was active in politics there. Sharma's two buses plied the route daily between Ranchi, Khunti and Jamshedpur. When Sharma came to see me at the clinic the first time, he had in his hand what looked like a wad of raffle tickets. But no, he was collecting donations for our local Hanuman temple and for organising devotional meetings during which the faithful would sing bhajans. He wrote out the amount you donated and gave it to you with a flourish that suggested you had bought a ticket to heaven.

Sharma was chewing paan and wearing a yellow polyester shirt unbuttoned at the top. He implied, or did he say it more explicitly, that I had enough money to support the community because I had carried out abortions.

But abortions had been legal for more than a decade! I don't think I pointed this out to Sharma in response. I guess I was numb with surprise or fright. A schoolteacher had recently come to me wanting an abortion because she said she had been raped by a colleague who taught physics at her school. She didn't want anyone to know. Had word got around? Did Sharma have something to do with what had happened to her? There was another case. A local railway official's wife, newly married, had also wanted an abortion. She said she would like to be able to tell her husband that she had suffered a miscarriage. I went ahead and did what she wanted.

Now, Sharma was sitting in my clinic making what seemed like a veiled threat. I felt I was being blackmailed just because I wanted to protect my patients. I stayed quiet for a few seconds, but Sharma was already trying a different method of attack. He said he was sure that my husband Ram supported his church, that the local Christian church had a lovely, shining dome, and wouldn't it be nice if I also supported the house of worship of my own faith. The Christian church got money from Germany, from the far-off United States, he said, how was Hinduism to survive without support either from outside or inside the country?

I found Anil Sharma bullying and insulting. I don't think I had ever met anyone who inspired so much anger in me even when he hadn't said a word yet. I think it had to do with his brazenness. He was a rude and unsavoury character. When he produced his badly printed pink ticket, I didn't want trouble and so I thought it better to pay a large amount and get rid of him. Our friend, the magistrate, was long gone. He had been promoted and had been given a desk job in Patna in the rural development department. I would have been ashamed to tell him what was happening in our town. Each Dussehra, I made the payment that Anil Sharma wanted and if there was some relief for me, it was that for several years, till Peter's death, Sharma didn't come to the clinic himself but sent Peter with that scrap of paper that looked like a raffle ticket and which I quickly threw away.

Maryam and I had both thought it funny that Peter had to change his name. Maryam is nothing if not a practical person and she accepted what Peter had done. What she hadn't expected, and what surprised her, was how Peter himself would change. He was ambitious, he was making money from his driving, and he wanted to please Sharma. I was told that on the six-to-eight-hour round trips on the bus each day, he would play for his passengers these cassettes of so-called holy men and women delivering fiery lectures on how Hindus had been crushed by Muslim invaders and their temples destroyed. Peter learned from these cassettes that after arriving on these shores the foreign missionaries had destroyed the culture of the Adivasi tribals by converting them to the Christian faith. His passengers heard these lectures too, and whether they believed it or not, Peter told Anil Sharma repeatedly that he understood that his return to Hinduism was indeed a homecoming.

During that time there were riots in parts of the country but not in Khunti. Although there was trouble in Jamshedpur and curfew was imposed also in Ranchi, we were left untouched.

Yet the following year, during Holi, there was a clash in town. A group of youths in a car threw colour on strangers in a lane and shouted slogans that led to a fight. It was a scuffle between Hindus and Muslims and, as the fighting heated up through the day, Anil Sharma and his men got involved. Peter too. I should tell you that Peter wasn't religious at all. The devotional meetings and bhajans were not for him. He liked that he had influence, and he certainly wanted power. I'm sure he entered the fray in order to play a role in the violence and emerge victorious. Unfortunately, the scuffle took a bad turn. A Hindu man lost an eye. By that night, everyone was in a frenzy.

I was told that Sharma was roaming the town in an open jeep haranguing small groups of Hindu youths to kill Muslims. An eye for an eye was the slogan now. Swords, spears, iron rods were put on display. The new magistrate, a young Sikh fellow, saw the conflict spilling out of control when Sharma's procession reached the Muslim area and the mob torched a police vehicle. The magistrate ordered the policemen to fire over the heads of the rioting mob. But a bullet found Peter. Overnight, he became a martyr.

For Maryam, there was the pain and grief of losing her brother. But what was a different kind of pain was that Peter was taken away from her and turned into a symbol. Despite the curfew, two men from Sharma's kirana store came to ask Maryam for a photograph of her brother. She gave it to them. In no time, the photograph had been enlarged, framed and garlanded. In the Hanuman Temple near the town's central chowk, the photograph sat on a wooden stool. Incense sticks lent the air a sickly sweet odour. A Hindu shrine had sprung up around Peter's framed portrait and the police didn't dare remove it. Anil Sharma had a new loudspeaker installed over the temple and people sang bhajans. The state elections were still eight months away and people began talking about how Sharma would be the most popular candidate from the area. Just around then I began hearing from my husband's students that he would make a good rival candidate but Ram dismissed the proposal. I hated the idea, sure that it would spell trouble.

—

The groom's party was now making an entry into the hotel. The doctor said that she would talk to me after we had witnessed the preliminary ceremony. We both moved with the crowd to greet the guests. A wide, curving ramp led from the pool to the path below where the groom's party had gathered. Satish's soon-to-be son-in-law's name was Paritosh. He was seated on a horse which stood at the bottom of the crowded ramp. A small stool with three steps had been placed by the animal's side but there was to be a wait as a few rituals needed to be performed. Paritosh worked for Google in San Francisco where he presumably used a car instead of a horse. I assumed that his life was distant from a past in which anyone dressed in a knee-length sherwani and wore a bejewelled sword at the waist. But he now sat astride the horse with those trappings and a tall magenta turban on his head. Over his face fell a curtain of small white jasmine blossoms: the groom, like a woman lifting a veil in a Rajasthani miniature, parted the strings of jasmine every two minutes to acknowledge a friend or a family member. His teeth were perfectly white and the impression of his smile lingered under the jasmine.

Did the doctor guess what I was thinking? Handsome boy, she said.

She was still looking at the groom. She added, Ram used to say that the difference between Christians and Hindus is that while Christians put a Christmas tree in their homes, the Hindus plant one on a horse and bring it home to marry their daughter.

That line belonged in an op-ed! *Dear editor, There is such unity in our difference...*

I said to Dr Ghosal, I would have enjoyed meeting Ram.

I spoke those words with great sincerity because I meant them. The doctor looked up at me, not out of surprise, but simply out of a sense of shared feeling, a feeling perhaps also of deep loss.

She said, It is very crowded here. Let's go back and sit down. I want to tell you a story about Ram.

Inside, in the lounge, the doctor began to speak again.

—

Ram was a complicated man, she said. I complained that the Adivasis were being fed lies by these people like Anil Sharma who distributed cassettes that distorted history. Ram must have been concerned but he was quite calm about it. He said that his hero Birsa Munda had told his followers that the guns of the British police would turn to wood and their bullets become water. Were they not lies? There is no field of politics where truth is a given and everyone agrees on it. For their part, Birsa's followers believed that the authorities couldn't arrest Birsa. He would turn into a log of wood. Even after his arrest, there were all sorts of rumours. That there was only a body of clay in the cell, Birsa had escaped and taken refuge in heaven.

I guess Ram was saying one couldn't be fanatical about truth, the doctor said.

She went on, I tried to argue with him. What about the conversions or counter-conversions – were they not attempts to spread hate? Here again he appeared unperturbed. If a man or woman saw reason to convert to Christianity, or for that matter, to Hinduism, if that is what it was that Anil Sharma wanted him to do, Ram thought it was okay. Birsa too had converted to Christianity and then gone back to his traditional Adivasi faith, worshipping his Bonga-Buru, and even then, his method of preaching was what he had learned in the Christian missions. Birsa was also influenced by the Vaishnav preachers and wore a dhoti dyed in turmeric and the sacred thread worn by many Hindus. And, let's not forget he also attacked the priesthood of the tribal bongas.

Ram's strategy was to always argue against a too rigid or what he called authoritarian definition of culture or history. In the public gatherings organised by newspapers or the district administration, he became a trickster figure embarrassing his opponents by pointing out how reality or our lived existence was so much richer than what their ideology dictated.

Ram had enemies on all sides. Once, Maryam reported that during a meeting in town Anil Sharma's brother from Jamshedpur had pointed to Ram's picture in the newspaper and asked why the caption didn't say that this was the poisonous snake of the forest, the Nag or the King Cobra. I didn't tell Ram this. He lived in his own world. He was trying to teach his students, poor and from a background without books, with limited resources in a provincial college, the writings of philosophers like Jacques Rancière and Michel Foucault. One summer he adapted, in both Hindi and Mundari, Hannah Arendt's *Eichmann in Jerusalem*. He was a great admirer of the novels of Albert Camus. I'm painting him as someone very serious. Ram would joke that he is exactly the kind of Adivasi that the government in Delhi wants to display on Republic Day. He would say, I'm a living, walking, talking, dancing stereotype. Ram loved the taste of mahua and would accept it at any hour of the day. And when he was really drunk, especially during festivals, he danced through the night.

People have become more aware of their rights; but I wonder whether we know more of our own history. Once at a gathering organised by a municipal councillor, Ram said that what had happened in the country during our first war of independence in 1857 had been inverted in recent times in the drive to build a temple at Ayodhya. When Ram presented this analysis, and was leaving the meeting, someone threw a brick at him. It hit his shoulder and I was just thankful it missed his head. I didn't look at the brick again but I was later told that these were special bricks with जय श्री राम written on them in Hindi. These bricks were headed to Ayodhya where they would be used to build a Ram temple.

—

I have told you so much, the doctor said. I should stop now.

The mention of the brick thrown at her husband's head had an ominous ring to it. I said, Doctor, if you don't mind me asking, how did Ram die?

She looked at me. We have been trained to talk about death, we are used to it, she said. But I'm tired. Let's talk tomorrow.

Satish has made me sign up for yoga with the bride's aunts. But I'll be free in the afternoon.

When I woke up in the morning, I was conscious that I had been dreaming. But I couldn't recall more than a detail or two. I was on a bus. There had been an accident on the road. I knew I was in India. While I was safe, maybe the bus or another vehicle had killed an animal. The passengers disembarked and there was a roadside dhaba nearby selling tea and sweets. Flies buzzed around the plates of sweets. I wanted to sip my tea but the milk had curdled and I threw it away.

With free time before me, I sat at my computer and searched for Ram Naresh Nag. I found a picture of him playing the flute. Then I saw a story with the headline 'Adivasi Scholar and Activist Murdered'. I didn't feel like reading the story. The temptation was strong but I decided I would return to it after I had spoken to the doctor. A few seconds passed. I asked myself if I should search online for the doctor's name. I hesitated because while the doctor knew that I was a writer I hadn't told her that I was already shaping a story about her in my head. She didn't know and most likely didn't even suspect that I was sitting in the hotel room contemplating searching online for the details of her life which I would then make public.

Promptly at three, as we had decided, I saw the doctor coming towards me in the hotel's restaurant. She looked altered, as if she has aged more during the night. Maybe it was only tiredness owing to travel and the setting. I got up from my chair and asked her if she was well.

No, she said plainly. But here we are.

She asked for tea.

As I watched the waiter pour the doctor's tea the thought that came to me, clearly and unexpectedly, was that of course she was the one who had brought me into the world. She was the only doctor – certainly the only gynaecologist – in Khunti. Who else would have helped my mother?

A silence grew between us.

Thank you for talking to me last night, I said to her after a while. You were telling me about your husband when we parted.

I remember, she said. I was thinking all night about what I wanted to tell you. I'm not a writer. It is not always easy to line up the past so that it leads to the present.

I waited when she fell silent and then she spoke again after gathering her thoughts.

—

When Ram died in March 1997, I kept doing my work at the clinic, even though I felt hollowed-out, not just alone but also very old. For the first time in my life, I felt exhausted. Maryam was my big support, never shirking her duties, and yet finding the resources to attend to me too. There were other blows. Three years after my husband's death, Adishankar, my assistant, discovered that he had cancer. All those years of smoking. We had worked together for close to thirty years. I was stricken. His wife had long been dead and the daughter who had been his life had been married for a few years. I looked at the X-rays and the report he brought from the oncologist in Ranchi. It looked bad. One month, three months? I told him that he should rest at home. We would take care of things in the clinic and we would also take care of him. He fell at my feet, crying. I thought he was afraid of a painful death – who wouldn't be? But no, he was asking for forgiveness.

I kept asking him what he wanted to apologise for, but for a long time I couldn't hear him above his crying.

He said that some men had come to his house one night during Dussehra, back when Ram was still alive. They had taken him to the home of an inspector in the Home Guards. The man's name was Suresh Yadav. Anil Sharma was there too. They were waiting for him. The policeman Yadav first asked Adishankar if he recognised Anil Sharma. Sharma was friendly at first. You do good work at the clinic, he said to Adishankar. You are going to get your daughter married off soon. If you need help, if you want to hire our guest house, let me know. We will give it to you cheaply.

Adishankar said he stood with his hands folded. No, *maalik*, I don't need anything, sir.

At which Anil Sharma laughed. He said to Adishankar, But I need something from you.

By now Adishankar had stopped crying. He could not meet my eyes. He still sat on the ground, and addressed my feet.

Anil Sharma had said to him that he needed to discuss the matter of Ram Naresh Nag. Sharma told Adishankar that he needed to talk to Ram for ten minutes in private. He had tried, he said, but not succeeded. This talk was necessary. It was urgent.

Sharma said, But you drive him sometimes from one place to another, don't you?

Adishankar began wailing now, the doctor said, but I don't know whether I could even hear him above the thumping of my own heart. After all these months and years, I was finally learning how Ram died.

The doctor said she made an attempt to come back to the present. Why didn't you tell me, Adishankar? Why didn't you tell the police?

He tried to touch my feet again.

Why? I must have been shouting by now, she said. He looked at me for the first time. He said, *Bola ki hamari beti ko uttha lega. Hum ko phir khali uska nanga body dekhne ko milega.* They said they would take my daughter away. That the next time I saw her it would be her naked corpse I would be looking at.

I didn't want to hear any more. I told Adishankar to go away. The very next day, the deputy superintendent of police and a magistrate went to his home. He gave a sworn statement describing how he had gone late one evening to Anil Sharma's shop and told him, while buying a prepaid calling card, that the next morning at eight he was to drive my new car to Tamar. There was no further conversation.

In the morning, Adishankar drove out with Ram. A few minutes after eight, just where the road splits left for Dasam Falls, two men stepped out on the road, waving down at the ground. Adishankar hadn't even come to a stop before they opened the doors and quickly got inside. One sat in the front and the other at the back. From what he heard the man in the backseat say, Adishankar could guess that the stranger was pointing a gun at Ram. The man in the front, maybe thirty-five years old, a *diku* with a light beard, slapped Adishankar.

Drive, *haraami* bastard.

They drove for five minutes before they asked Adishankar to stop and wait on the other side of the road for a bus that would bring him back to Khunti. Adishankar told the magistrate that he had taken the bus as directed and he had come to report the matter to me at the clinic.

I should tell you what happened when Adishankar had

made his sudden appearance that morning, looking wild-eyed, telling me how two strangers had taken Ram away. I called the superintendent of police, a young and decent man named Menon. He said he would alert the police at the checkpoints on all highways. He also sent me his official jeep to bring me to the police station. By the time I reached there, Menon and his team were getting ready to leave.

Please wait here, Menon said to me. We have received some information. Would you like tea?

I said I didn't want tea. I told Menon, You will have to take me with you. Please.

Did we drive outside town for fifteen minutes? Twenty? The driver had switched on the siren in the jeep and I found the noise deafening. There was no conversation among the men. Then, a man seated in the back said, Yes, drive to the left. I can see it.

I could see nothing. My car, which I had bought six months earlier, was a red Maruti. The police jeep drew close to a car that was a mix of pale brown and grey. About twenty villagers stood nearby. Speaking either to me or his constables, the superintendent of police said, *Dekhiye, metal bahut garam hoga.* The metal will be very hot.

I'm a doctor. It seems I see death every day. But this was new to me. The glass on the windows of the car had exploded or melted, I don't know, and I was to believe that instead of a tall man with beautiful, nearly shoulder-length hair, the charred, unrecognisable skeleton inside was my husband. No. The police officer's hand was on my arm, but I only wanted to say no. Can you be sure? It was only a minute ago, well, just that morning that I had seen Ram wearing a light-blue, half-sleeve shirt, and a navy-blue vest. This sounds terrible but I thought they had set

103

fire to a short Adivasi man – Mundas aren't tall, though Ram was. He also had lighter skin. How could Ram have shrunk like this? Instead of my red car there was this ash-brown thing – except that you could see flecks of still-red paint in the front, especially in the middle of the hood.

Everyone was standing back. In my mind, or maybe even out loud, I kept saying No, no. Instead of this no, all the silent people around me were waiting for me to say yes and to make it all real for them. But does horror become real because you are told that they had locked the doors of the Maruti before throwing a burning rag in the fuel tank? No. It never became real to me. And it never became real enough for others either. So three years after the crime had been committed, on the basis of a dying man's confession, the government authorities arrested Anil Sharma. His lawyer argued that the case was baseless and, besides, his client was suffering from diabetes and should be released. Sharma was in prison for two months and then the government accepted defeat. No other witness would come forward; the police never found the men who had abducted Ram in the car and then murdered him; the defence produced witnesses who exonerated Sharma. Adishankar also died. During his last days, I took care of him – I was helped by his daughter who had meant the world to him when he was alive.

Dear Editor, There is no justice, just us.

—

The doctor was catching a flight to Delhi, and then after spending two days there she was going to board a flight to Ranchi. I knew I would never see her again. She had been generous, extremely so, in talking to me, a stranger. Was I being vain in imagining that she had narrated her story to a writer so that it could be shared with others? I waited another day. Then, sitting down at my computer I searched online for her name. There was nothing except a link on the *Dainik Jagran* website, in the regional Jharkhand issue of the Hindi paper, a report from some years back. A small, not very consequential report, and yet, I felt it important to extend our conversation further just a bit. Perhaps distance or time would provide a different conclusion to our story. To emphasise this point, I sent the doctor an email inquiring, in the manner of the conventional journalistic interviewer, whether she had any regrets about her past. I also asked her to comment on the newspaper report. I told her I would write a report called 'Narsing Medical' about how a remote town fell under the sway of a violent and extremist way of thinking. I wasn't sure how good a correspondent she would be but after four days I saw her reply in my inbox.

Under the subject line Re: Narsing Medical, she had written, I am happy to have had the chance to talk to you. In the normal course of my life, given the pace of work, and the wretched conditions in which people around me survived, it is impossible and even unnecessary to examine one's motives. I have not been a character in my story, but you made me see myself as one in what I was telling you.

The news item you have mentioned refers to the death of a thirty-year-old woman in my clinic. It is accurate in telling us that she had lost a child in an accident at the Panchghagh Falls. What is its point? That a woman who had suffered a calamity was then not saved at my clinic? I cannot speculate on the motives. The reporter was searching, if you pardon the pun, for a cause.

What he has missed is the extraordinary events that happened prior to the woman's tragic death. The woman's child was three years old. He fell into the water when his mother's foot slipped on a rock at the Panchghagh. The water moves very fast there. It was Christmas and so there was a big crowd at the waterfalls. But others got involved too. All along the narrow river, at regular intervals, ten or twelve men formed a slow-moving line, everyone joined by a rope they held in their hands, using their feet as net to catch the boy. They found the child's body, so that the parents' agony could find a resting place. Even in that short time, the river fish had already eaten his eyes and the father said that the boy's eyes had been received by the river goddess. I was just impressed that long before the police could act, the people had got together and helped find the boy.

The mother was brought to the clinic because she was in pain. She was clutching her stomach. Her brother felt that she had hurt herself during her fall. But the woman told me that this pain, nearly unbearable, had been with her for several days. The smallest pressure on her abdomen where the appendix is located made her cry out in pain. There was no time to lose. I asked Maryam to prepare her for surgery. But it was too late. Her appendix had already ruptured, the abdominal cavity was severely inflamed, and the infection had spread. We gave her antibiotics but to no avail. She was also anaemic. A history of abdominal disorders as well as her recent attack of pneumonia suggested a weak immune system. I couldn't save her.

I am a doctor. My job is to heal. What has perplexed me so much all my life as a healer is that I have seen the most violent, the most brutal people, I'm talking now of those who have the actual power, act as if they are the ones carrying the biggest wound in their histories and in their hearts. Can you please explain this to me?

If I was conceited about my work, or particularly stupid, I would imagine that the good doctor was asking me to write an op-ed. But that is not what she was asking. I returned to the rest of her email.

When I look at these people, she wrote, and some of our leaders are among them, I feel that theirs is a wound I can never heal because there is no medicine for bad faith. These are people who are lying to others and they are also lying to themselves. No mirror in the world can show them their true face. And at the end of the day, this knowledge is the only medicine I now have.

You have asked me if I have any regrets. In my professional life? No. In my personal life? Yes. I wish I could have saved Ram.

Less than three years after Ram was killed, there were riots in Gujarat. Everyone knows of the two thousand Muslims murdered by mobs of zealots but there was a Hindu woman killed in the riots who has a near-sacred place in my heart. I read about her in the papers. Her name was Geetaben. She was lynched in Ahmedabad, her clothes torn off, her head bashed in with a brick. They did this to her because she was trying to defend her Muslim lover. They gave a Bharat Ratna award to the man who was prime minister at that time, and there were no awards for the dead woman, and, one could add, no help for her either. So, please, put that at the top of my list of regrets. I regret not being there, as a woman, as a citizen, and as a Hindu, although I don't know what that even means these days, to help Geetaben. I regret not having been Geetaben for Ram.

New Titles from Giramondo

Fiction

Jon Fosse *Septology* (trans. Damion Searls)

Shaun Prescott *Bon and Lesley*

George Alexander *Mortal Divide: The Autobiography of Yiorgos Alexandroglou*

Luke Carman *An Ordinary Ecstasy*

Norman Erikson Pasaribu *Happy Stories, Mostly* (trans. Tiffany Tsao)

Jessica Au *Cold Enough for Snow*

Max Easton *The Magpie Wing*

Zarah Butcher-McGunnigle *Nostalgia Has Ruined My Life*

Pip Adam *Nothing to See*

Non-fiction

Bastian Fox Phelan *How to Be Between*

Antigone Kefala *Late Journals*

Evelyn Juers *The Dancer: A Biography for Philippa Cullen*

Gerald Murnane *Last Letter to a Reader*

Anwen Crawford *No Document*

Vanessa Berry *Gentle and Fierce*

Poetry

Lucy Dougan *Monster Field*

Michael Farrell *Googlecholia*

Lisa Gorton *Mirabilia*

Zheng Xiaoqiong *In the Roar of the Machine* (trans. Eleanor Goodman)

Lionel Fogarty *Harvest Lingo*

Tracy Ryan *Rose Interior*

Claire Potter *Acanthus*

Adam Aitken *Revenants*

J.S. Harry *New and Selected Poems*

Andy Jackson *Human Looking*

Eunice Andrada *Take Care*

Jane Gibian *Beneath the Tree Line*

For more information visit giramondopublishing.com.

Subscribe Now
And receive each issue of HEAT
Australia's international literary magazine

Since its inception in 1996, HEAT has been renowned for a dedication to quality
and a commitment to publishing innovative and imaginative poetry, fiction,
essays and hybrid forms. Now, in the third series, we bring together a selection
of the most interesting and adventurous Australian and overseas writers. HEAT
is posted to subscribers every two months, forming a unique, cohesive whole.
Your subscription supports independent literary publishing, and enables us to
cultivate and champion new and challenging writing.

Visit giramondopublishing.com/heat/ to subscribe.

Submission Guidelines
HEAT welcomes submissions of fiction, essays, poetry and translated works
throughout the year. We encourage writing which gives full rein to the author's
voice, without the restriction of a word limit. In the case of poetry, we seek
longer poems, or a selection or sequence of poems. For further information,
please visit our website.

Acknowledgements

We respectfully acknowledge the Gadigal, Burramattagal and Cammeraygal peoples, the traditional owners of the lands where Giramondo's offices are located. We extend our respects to their ancestors and to all First Nations peoples and Elders.

HEAT Series 3 Number 6 has been prepared in collaboration with Ligare Book Printers, Avon Graphics, Ball & Doggett paper suppliers and Candida Stationery; we thank them for their support.

The Giramondo Publishing Company is grateful for the support of Western Sydney University in the implementation of its book publishing program.

Giramondo Publishing is assisted by the Australian Government through the Australia Council for the Arts.

HEAT Series 3
Editor Alexandra Christie
Designer Jenny Grigg
Typesetter Andrew Davies
Copyeditor Aleesha Paz
Marketing and Publicity Manager Kate Prendergast
Publishers Ivor Indyk and Evelyn Juers
Associate Publisher Nick Tapper

Editorial Advisory Board
Chris Andrews, Mieke Chew, J.M. Coetzee, Lucy Dougan, Lisa Gorton,
Bella Li, Tamara Sampey-Jawad, Suneeta Peres da Costa, Alexis Wright
and Ashleigh Young.

Contact
For editorial enquiries, please email
heat.editor@giramondopublishing.com.
Follow us on Instagram @HEAT.lit and
Twitter @HEAT_journal.

Accessibility
We understand that some formats will not be accessible to all readers.
If you are a reader with specific access requirements, please contact
orders@giramondopublishing.com.

For more information, visit giramondopublishing.com/heat.

Published December 2022
from the Writing and Society Research Centre
at Western Sydney University
by the Giramondo Publishing Company
Locked Bag 1797
Penrith NSW 2751 Australia
www.giramondopublishing.com

This collection © Giramondo Publishing 2022
Typeset in Tiempos and Founders Grotesk Condensed
designed by Kris Sowersby at Klim Type Foundry

Printed and bound by Ligare Book Printers
Distributed in Australia by NewSouth Books

A catalogue record for this book is available from
the National Library of Australia.

HEAT Series 3 Number 6
ISBN: 978-1-922725-05-9
ISSN: 1326-1460

ISBN 978-1-922725-05-9

9 781922 725059 >